The Way It Was With Me

To my old friend, Brian Desmond Hurst,
as a slight token of my affection and respect

The author

The Way It Was With Me

Gerald Hamilton

LESLIE FREWIN : LONDON

BY THE SAME AUTHOR:

Desert Dreamers
As Young as Sophocles
Mr Norris and I
Emma in Blue
Jacaranda
Blood Royal

First published by Leslie Frewin Publishers Limited,
One New Quebec Street, Marble Arch, London W1

This book is set in Imprint,
printed by Anchor Press
and bound by William Brendon,
both of Tiptree, Essex

09 096560 4

Contents

Acknowledgements

I MUST EXPRESS my deep gratitude to those periodicals, such as *The New Statesman*, *The Spectator* and *Punch*, who have allowed me to quote from their columns, and for the assistance given to me by various friends.

I wish to express my warmest thanks to my good friend, James Pope-Hennessy, for being so extremely kind as to write the Foreword for this book, despite his being so very busy an author.

I particularly wish to thank Gillian Mansel for the great help she has given me and for her patience. Without her assistance this book would never have been completed.

I must thank Peter Burton for his skill in research and the help he has given me.

Finally, I would like to thank Mr Graham Murray for permission to quote from *The Sword and the Umbrella*, and Mr Anthony Gibbs for permission to quote from *Mr Norris and I*.

GH, CHELSEA

August 1969

Foreword

SINCE THE AUTHOR of this book is in many ways unique he clearly cannot be classified. Yet, though Gerald Hamilton fits into no general catalogue of the human race, he does belong to a select and interesting class of personages – those who are reputed to have served as prototypes for certain famous characters in English fiction. In Gerald's case it is, of course, Arthur Norris in Christopher Isherwood's *Mr Norris Changes Trains*.

Now, for a living person to be known far and wide as the original of some immortal fictional character may be very flattering, but surely it must have its drawbacks. In my view the chief of these would be the stranger's wish, so often expressed in Gerald's particular instance, to be introduced to 'the *real* Mr Norris'. It is not, I think, everyone who would care to be known to the world in this guise, but Gerald Hamilton takes it in good part, and is even, I suspect, flattered by it. None the less, for outsiders he will ever remain Mr Norris, and they will not try to peer behind the mask to find the *real* Mr Hamilton – intelligent, intolerant, kindly, excellent company, always prepared to amuse or to be amused – an octogenarian defying fate with his hat at a jaunty angle. This candid and zestful volume of reminiscences could never have been written by Mr Arthur Norris.

A patriotic Irishman born eighty-one years ago in Shanghai, Gerald Hamilton has led a peripatetic life of political intrigue and entertaining adventure, much of which is recorded in these present memoirs. Like its author, the book bristles with contradiction and prejudice. A staunch monarchist, a Tory so die-hard as to seem antediluvian, his attitude to Irish questions has ever been violently radical and republican. His views on Ireland will be found here, as well as some of his more virulent and often justified prejudices – that against smoking, for example, a habit he regards as not only barbarous in itself, but totally destructive of a palate for wine.

The Way It Was With Me is, moreover, filled with vignettes of those he has known in the past – ranging from his friend Roger Casement to Rasputin, whom he watched curing an epileptic. This book is likewise illuminated by shafts of the author's special form of humour. Gerald Hamilton, in fact, has managed to bring off a feat which few contemporary writers of their own reminiscences seem able to achieve – he has thrown himself down on paper heart and soul. Reading *The Way It Was With Me* is as good as hearing him talk.

JAMES POPE-HENNESSY

August 1969

Chapter One

London As I Remember It

If any god should say
'I will restore
The world her yesterday
Whole as before
My judgment blasted it', who would not lift
Heart, eye, and hand in passion o'er the gift?

Rudyard Kipling

I WOULD LIKE to refer to the difference between the happy days of my childhood and youth and the horror of life in London today. It must be remembered that when I was a boy telephones were practically non-existent and so were typewriters and other essentials of today's life. Motor cars at the beginning of the century were viewed with horror and dismay by the horsey people of the day. Carriage horses invariably shied when they met a motor car on the road and I became quite adept at jumping out of the carriage before anyone else could do so while the horses reared! In the happy placid London before the First World War invitations would be sent by hand – as a rule by maids or footmen, who could be seen scurrying about all over London bearing messages.

I personally enjoyed travelling by hansom cab, the jingle of the bells and the cheerfulness of the cab driver always delighted my boyish heart. I remember too that invitations to dinner at that time, often printed, bore in the corner the notice: 'Carriages at 10.30 pm', or maybe at 11 pm – eleven o'clock was quite late in those days. When I was first taken to dinner parties I remember, if those relatives who had brought me were anxious to go, when the butler announced that the carriage had come, he or she would

9

jump up at once. 'Oh, my dear, I cannot possibly keep the horses waiting in this cold, so I am afraid I must say "goodbye".' On the other hand, if the evening was being really enjoyed, he or she would say: 'Is it so late already! I wonder if my coachman could have a glass of beer in your servants' hall with your butler and I shall be ready in half an hour.' The whole system of the servants at the turn of the century was a kind of puzzle in itself. As is well known, private maids or valets were always called in the servants' hall by the name of their master or mistress, but there was a special hierarchy and the butler, the housekeeper, the lady's maid and master's valet usually ate together and the rest of the servants separately.

Country-house visits were great occasions and though it has been said that a bell was always rung in the morning about eight so that when the maid brought the morning tea the visitors were always found in their right beds, I have never personally known the bell to ring in the many houses where I have stayed. Servants at the turn of the century were always plentiful and I remember a parlour maid being threatened with dismissal if a mistake occurred again saying, 'Oh no, madam, please not that'.

Servants had particular duties to perform and one would never perform the duties of another. One afternoon I happened to be calling on Lady Howard of Glossop when she remarked that the room seemed cold and she asked me to 'touch the bell as the fire requires another lump of coal'. I did so. The stately butler appeared and when told what was wanted, bowed and retired. A little later a footman appeared and solemnly placed two lumps of coal on the fire. Lady Howard had a lovely house in Rutland Gate and I remember she and her husband always had numerous guests, all of whom possessed the grand manner and were generous, proud and jovial, but not really happy. On the question of food and drink, I will wait until a later chapter to discuss Edwardian meals and above all Edwardian drinks. Edward VII made a strict rule that no drinks of any kind should be served before a meal because he was absolutely convinced that they only served to dull the palate and threatened the enjoyment of good wines. The menus were always written in French and were translated into English for the staff with notes about the wines to be served with each course. I particularly remember that in all great houses at the end of a meal two or sometimes three vintage ports were served to each guest; the guest then chose the one he liked best and had that glass refilled. What particularly interested me was how the footmen's powdered hair remained so firm and the powder never seemed to fall into the soup!

There followed always the important ritual of the visiting cards. Guests were expected to leave cards on their host and hostess within about three days of the dinner. It is true that more often than not servants were sent with the cards, but if one wanted to be polite, instead of sending cards they were delivered personally by the guest or guests with the top right-hand corner turned down. There was a kind of agreement at the time that nobody would cheat at this silly game! I have noticed the custom continue in Madrid quite recently.

Everybody alive today who remembers this epoch will recall the joy of going to the theatre when in all West End theatres full evening dress was *de rigueur* and ladies wore their most beautiful *toilettes*. It was the day of the stage-door johnnies and if I thought long enough I ought to be able to remember many of the happiest marriages into the peerage of contemporary actresses and chorus girls. I remember, for instance, Rosie Boote being engaged to Lord Headfort, the head of the Taylour family, and what a happy marriage that was. I can even remember the lines in a music-hall song of the time:

> *Molly married a Marquess,*
> *What a thing to do,*
> *She took him down to country town*
> *And hurried the service through –*

and so it went on. The lady I knew best, of course, was Gertie Millar, who married Lionel Monckton, the most successful song writer of the time. They had a lovely house in Russell Square and at one time I was invited on most Sundays to go there for lunch. Old Lady Monckton, Lionel's mother, was the widow of a former

Lord Mayor of London and she was a remarkably amusing old lady. She never would say 'I went to the theatre', but always 'I went to the play': Later, of course, after Lionel Monckton's death, Gertie Millar married Lord Dudley and both her marriages were happy and successful. Once in Paris in the twenties I found myself sitting next to her in the theatre and I hesitated to make myself known, thinking that there had been a gap of so many years since last seeing her, but she recognised me and I was very happy that she should do so. I think the London of this period was just as immoral as it is today, but much less openly so. The 11th Commandment 'Thou shalt not be found out' was assiduously obeyed, but terrible scandals did occasionally break out. The Prince of Wales, for instance, being cited in a divorce case as co-respondent shook London, and various homosexual raids followed by criminal prosecutions were quite frequent. If, however, any of those involved had a respected name, he was invariably allowed to escape abroad, as in the case of Lord Henry Somerset who went to live in Florence, where I first met him. Other cases had their tragic and sad endings, such as the suicide of General Sir Hector MacDonald in a Paris hotel. One must remember that at this time the Wilde scandal was only about ten years old.

It was during the beginning of the reign of Edward VII that the Jewish influence began to be felt. As a young man I could not resist making up some brief lines about this:

> I do admire
> Lady Speyer.
> She's always climbing
> Higher and higher.
> I am very fond
> Of Lady Mond
> But can I aspire
> To Adèle Meyer?

And as to the London season when everybody who considered themselves anybody was expected to be in London from May until the end of July each year, I ventured a short rhyme which ran:

Sir Archibald and Lady Blane
Have struggled up to town again,
And this that London folk might see
Their hefty daughter, Dorothy.
Sir Archie in his Club all day
Thinks of the bills he'll have to pay.
His wife is bored and hates the smell
Of cooking in her small hotel.
While Dolly in the season's swing
Thinks of the Shropshire woods in spring,
And of a dog tied up at home, poor thing.
Poor thing!!

Now the scene changes and I turn to the London of today. The difference between the gracious city during the first years of this century and of the overcrowded London of today would seem to be almost indescribable, were it not unfortunately so true. The first casualty in this 'brave new world' seems to have been manners. Are there any left? Even public transport is unpleasant, the dreary sad faces that confront one in buses or tubes have on me a most depressing effect. In the old days as a young man I often used to climb on to the top of a horse bus and engage in conversation the driver, if I managed to get a place on the front seat. I learned a tremendous amount from these conversations.

I do not wish to dwell too long on the unhappy difference between the two Londons and to those people who always say 'It was all very well for the rich in the old days, but what about the poor?' I can only say that the poor were as well looked after as can be expected, not so much by the lady bountifuls of the day, as by charitably disposed families who took a personal, even an affectionate interest in the welfare of each of the many servants they may have had. The great cook, Soyer, who cooked at the Reform Club after having been cook to the Royal Family in France, was so appalled at the famine in Ireland in 1848 that, at his own expense, he went to Ireland with a special stove he had invented, later used in the Crimean War, and prepared soup all over the country. Various highly placed people left him large sums in their wills to continue this good work. The absentee landlords were, of course, responsible for the misery, but it is interesting to show that even in Ireland the very poor were never quite neglected. Many society ladies joined Soyer in his enterprise and he gave to these ladies private classes instructing them how to make nourishing soups for what were then called 'the hungry poors'. On the death of one of these ladies, the family were somewhat startled to learn from the solicitor in charge of her estate that ample funds had been set aside to supply the poor of her parish 'with a brothel to be named after her'. It was only when the solicitor opened an envelope marked in an elegant sloping Victorian hand 'Three recipes for excellent broth for my brothel' that they realised what the good lady's intentions were.

Chapter Two

China – the Land of My Birth

MY DEEP AFFECTION for China, the land of my birth, has never waned. I was born in Shanghai, but on my mother's death was shipped off to my mother's parents, under the care of two Chinese amahs; but after my schooldays at Rugby, my one ambition was to return to the land of my birth, which I was able to do at the age of twenty. The China of those days was, of course, very different from what it so quickly became. There was complete safety for travellers throughout the immense empire and the Imperial Government in Pekin knew precisely how to rule this enormous country of, at that time, between five and six hundred million.

I had a great regard for the Dowager Empress, who was ailing when I arrived in China, and admired her skill in playing off one aggressive European government against another in much the same manner as did the Sultan Abdul Hamid of Turkey. Of course I never saw the Dowager Empress, but was in Pekin in October 1908 and able to watch her funeral procession and that of the young Emperor. It was not a very spectacular occasion and the procession was very straggly. The Chief Eunuch carried the Empress's little dog, Moo-tan (Chinese for Paeony), in front of the Imperial bier. It was a yellow-and-white Pekinese with a white spot on its forehead.

Quite recently – that is to say in 1965 – there was a great deal of correspondence in various newspapers detrimental to the Dowager

15

Empress, who was accused of murdering the Pearl Concubine with whom the young Emperor was so much in love. The late Robert Pitman raised this point in the *Sunday Express* and I saw a copy of the paper and wrote at once as follows:

> I was privileged in 1908 to meet the Chief Imperial Eunuch and can claim to have become a close friend of his. I was assured by him that what really happened was that when the Imperial Family decided to leave Pekin (this was at the time of the Boxer Rebellion) the Empress forbade her weak-willed nephew the Emperor to allow the Pearl Concubine to accompany them, as she was jealous of this lady's increasing power.
> The Pearl Concubine, who really loved the Emperor with great passion, committed suicide (thinking she would never see him again) by jumping into a deep well. It is obvious that had the Empress wished to murder this Concubine, she could have done so in a much less spectacular fashion than by throwing her down a well.

It must be remembered that the Boxer Rebellion had only been over six or seven years and the crimes committed by the European troops, especially the looting of the treasures in the Winter Palace and the Summer Palace, were not yet forgiven.

I had managed to make the acquaintance of the Chief Imperial Eunuch, although he spoke no English and I at that time no Chinese, but my wonderful interpreter, who accompanied me on all my travels in China – Wu Ting Chang – was both tactful and made friends easily. I was able to see the Empress's Pekinese dogs, which seemed to be quite different from those one meets with in Europe. They were much smaller, not aggressive, but very dignified in their approach to strangers.

In the early part of the century Sir Robert Hart was in charge of the Imperial Customs. He had been accorded a Chinese mandarin's title and spoke the most perfect Chinese that any foreigner has ever spoken. He was very fond of China and served the Imperial Dynasty with love and affection, and I felt it was a great honour for me to have met him.

Various 'attractions' were offered me in Pekin, notably the suggestion that I should watch a public execution of some fifty or sixty robbers and bandits. Naturally, I did not wish to attend this, but was appalled and shocked by the number of laughing foreigners who hurried to the field where the beheadings took place.

In my estimation, the whole relationship between foreigners and the Chinese was utterly wrong. Europeans looked down on the Chinese as if they were an inferior race, when of course their wonderful civilisation – perhaps the most wonderful in the world, not forgetting Rome and Greece – showed them to be in most respects superior in every way to the foreign intruders. I use the word intruders because the Treaty Ports had been fairly recently opened to foreign traders – partly as a result of the so-called opium war when Canton was bombarded by the British Fleet to force the Emperor of the time to admit the importation of opium, which was strictly forbidden under three separate Imperial edicts. Of course, opium has done more harm to China than the many depredations of the foreign intruders.

I returned to Shanghai, which I was making my headquarters, partly because I not only had many friends there, but also relatives of my family. Entertaining in Shanghai was done sumptuously. The houses, larger and roomier than Western dwellings, were admirably adapted to enormous gatherings. Money was spent with a far greater profusion than in the West and, as vast fortunes were made and lost in the course of a few weeks on the Shanghai Stock Exchange, hostesses vied with each other in offering repasts which would have seemed ostentatiously vulgar to the European eye. The cost of living was very much cheaper than in England; only imported articles of Western manufacture were expensive. Wine was duty free, and champagne was always offered to a guest either in the morning or in the afternoon after tennis. I had often to open a dozen bottles during a single day to offer to casual callers. The richer merchants of Shanghai brought magnificent horses from Europe, and their equipages, with sometimes one or two 'mafoos' in bright livery standing behind the carriage, ready to jump down and open the door, or drive away pedestrians, gave these vehicles a positively regal appearance. Everybody, even the European shop assistants, had one or two Manchu ponies to ride; otherwise the usual mode of conveyance was the humble ricsha, and even the ricshas in Shanghai seemed more up to date than elsewhere in the East. Some of them at that time had pneumatic tyres and cushion seats.

As everywhere else in the East, the standard of living amongst foreigners was considerably higher and the standard of morals considerably lower than in Europe. Bachelors lived openly with Japanese women (a Chinese prostitute was even in the Treaty Ports a *rara avis* at that time, and in the interior quite unknown), and no one found anything unusual in this arrangement, which was varied by occasional affairs with an Eurasian typist or with a married European lady. Even the husbands of Shanghai accompanied the bachelors on their frequent excursions 'down the line' – the row of large houses at the corner of the Kiangse Road and the canal, inhabited by American ladies who sold their favours for the established price of fifteen Mexican dollars; this did not include the vast amount of champagne absorbed by the visitors and the ladies of the house. Payment was made not in ready money, but by a 'chit', the client signing his name and the sum owed on a piece of paper placed ready on the hall table when he left. The system of 'chits' was in practice in every shop store and business house; they were presented punctually on the first of every month at the office of the debtor. Naturally this system was a strong inducement to extravagance and prodigality; yet I seldom heard of a 'chit' being refused or not honoured.

Friends used to mock me because I once said I wanted to make the acquaintance of the Chinese and received the reply: 'Whatever next! How absurd you are! Fancy calling on the Chinese!' I did not dare at the time to state that I not only intended to learn the Chinese language (mandarin), but to wear Chinese costume, which is not only prettier but much healthier than English attire. The study of the Chinese language and customs revealed a new world to me. China presented to my eager and admiring gaze the amazing spectacle of a *civilisation arrêtée*. The civilisations of Babylon and Egypt, of Greece and Rome, had risen, waned and disappeared, and the world they left behind them was no better for their brilliant passage. The Chinese civilisation, having reached, as it seemed to my enthusiastic temperament, the state nearest to perfection that it is possible to attain on this planet, had remained at the point it had reached four thousand years ago, arrested in its further progress by the fear of a complete collapse.

The definition of the word 'civilisation' is a task I am not competent to attempt; still, when a satisfactory definition is found, I hope it may include some reference to the instinctive subconscious communion of the spirit with the Infinite. No Chinaman, however lowly his calling, is entirely without this attribute. Naturally the most obvious vehicle of communion is by way of the fine arts, and the sublime art of China stands unique today before the world.

We Westerners, aglow with ready insolence and fatuous ambitions, because we have invented means of locomotion too rapid for any old-fashioned Chinaman to care to adopt, because our sanitary arrangements may be considered perhaps superior to those in general use in China, because we wallow in a materialism that not only to any Chinaman but to any Easterner is positively revolting, permit ourselves to suppose that we stand on a higher cultural level than the Chinaman. As a matter of fact, our own accepted philosophers are eager to assure us that our own precious civilisation is completely false, useless, and *verkehrt*. But even without the aid of a philosopher, it ought to be sufficiently obvious to any thinking Westerner that so long as we continue to extend the crown of laurels and the greatest honours of the State to the destroyers instead of to the preservers of the human race, there must be something very wrong with our moral outlook; so long as great soldiers receive the tributes of the multitude, while doctors and artists are allowed to live and die obscurely (with almost ridiculously rare exceptions), then we have but little right to preach to others.

And preach we do. 'First the missionary, then the gunboat, then the land-grabbing, that is the modern history of China,' said a Cambridge educated Chinaman to me. What he said was only the bitter truth then. The swarms of missionaries, belonging to each and all of the several Protestant denominations which infested every province of China, spreading confusion and hatred and encouraging the pretensions of their supposed converts, must have been an object of aversion and mistrust to every thinking Chinaman. Very poorly educated, often fanatical young men, always with large families, used to hurry out to China from Europe and America with a genuine intention of reforming and Christian-ising a people who had attained their admittedly high state of civilisation ages before the fusion of races which produced that to which the teacher belonged, when his remote ancestors, clad only in woad, settled their differences with clubs.

Finding his efforts to convert the 600,000,000 of Chinese utterly useless, the Protestant missionary divided his activity between spreading the basest libels against the Roman Catholic Church (which did claim some measure of success); supporting the preposterous claims of some interested convert, a so-called 'Rice Christian', who had nominally accepted baptism in order to be sure of the help of his missionary's consul in some dispute; or fomenting those disorders which his government would surely know how to profit by, even if he did not. I must attest, however, that I was privileged to meet, and during my different journeys into the interior to accept the hospitality of, several magnificent exceptions – but such exceptions were indeed rare.

However, viewed through European spectacles, China was the country of topsy-turvydom: It is the land where white was the colour of mourning and red of rejoicing, where men wore skirts and women trousers, where a saucer was placed over and not under a cup, where when greeting a friend one shook one's own hand warmly, where a title went backwards to the ancestors instead of forward to the offspring, where people paid their doctors only as long as they remained in good health. Also the country where my Number One Boy, Kwei Ching, appeared one day with bright yellow European shoes and leggings under his usual blue robe. They looked so ugly and unsuitable that at last I commented on them, but he replied evasively: 'Yesterday's rice is eaten and finished. Yesterday's tea is drunk and the leaves scattered. Today we must prepare a new dinner to be ready for the morrow.' Why, if he was anxious to move with the times he would sacrifice only his shoes on the altar of modernity, I was never able to find out.

After six months of Shanghai I decided to go to Japan to spend the summer there. Kwei Ching was all agog at the prospect of the journey and asked a dozen times, 'And shall this dust-like one be allowed to accompany the Glory of the East on his journey to the monkey islands?' I replied that of course I needed him with me.

One evening when I returned after dinner to my apartment just before we sailed, Kwei Ching, smiling as usual, and with a great air of mystery, followed me into my bedroom and said, 'Tonight the Protector of the Poor will be pleased with his servant Kwei Ching.' Drawing aside some curtains he revealed to my astonished gaze three tittering Japanese maidens, who in their gay kimonos looked for all the world like three butterflies in a sombre cage of mahogany.

As I expected that the damsels would surely understand Chinese, I said to Kwei Ching in pidgin-English (a language he detested), 'Boy, what thing you do? Who man tellee catchee girl? My no wantchee girl. My belong bobbery.' Kwei Ching's smiles vanished, and he answered in Chinese with what dignity he could muster, 'Let the Shelter of the World but cast his eyes a moment upon these three pieces of contentment. If one or other of them has the good fortune to find favour, let her remain, and maybe the Most Merciful Lord would care to take her on his journey to the monkey islands.'

I must admit I could not help laughing. I knew it was the fashion for every unmarried European to drag one or more Japanese women about with him on his travels in the Far East. Still, I had no intention of starting a harem, and so told Kwei Ching to get rid of the ladies without wounding their susceptibilities, and to give a dollar or two to each. As Kwei Ching was undressing me he said, 'The Consolation of his Ancestors is always right – untrustworthy feminines are as plentiful as tea-leaves in a tea-house, and if one should be needed, this miserable one will surely find the least ugly and conduct her to the Defender of the Afflicted.'

The country life in Japan, off the beaten track, was simple and idyllic, and the peasants very clean. Up-country in China I had seen dirt and squalor indescribable, and few indeed were the Chinese who could be persuaded to spend even one night in any of the so-called 'rest-houses', where the multitude of fleas, bugs and insects of all kinds prevented the hardiest traveller from enjoying a moment's repose. And yet, and yet . . . There was something in China, indefinite and yet very real, that made almost every unbiased traveller to the Far East prefer China to Japan, and the

Chinese to the Japanese. What it was I cannot say; but it was there, and few indeed were those who did not appreciate it.

I visited various Chinese cities of interest, going to Tientsin by boat, and thence to Pekin by rail. Nankin, Chinkiang, Soochow, being on the railway, were easy to reach from Shanghai. I also visited Hankow and went up the Yangtze as far as Ichang. The faithful Kwei Ching accompanied me on all my journeys. Somewhat to his annoyance, I had engaged as 'Number Two Boy' one Ah Sung, who was as graceful and handsome as poor Kwei Ching was the reverse. Ah Sung was supposed to assist Kwei Ching in the apartment I had, but just as he spent all his money on buying fine silks and clothes, so he spent most of his time posing in front of one of the large mirrors in my bedroom. 'Gazelle eyes' (for that was the translation of Ah Sung's nickname) had been destined for the stage as an actor of female parts, but he had been, while still a lad of thirteen, kidnapped by an elderly mandarin who lived at Nankin, and from whom he managed to escape.

It was in Nankin I first saw him and, struck by his unusual beauty, I agreed at his request to engage him as 'Number Two Boy'. Naturally a fierce rivalry existed between him and Kwei Ching, who would allow no hotel servant to minister to my wants. Still, each in his different way showed me an affection and a devotion I was very far from deserving. Kwei Ching detested foreigners and all their works; Ah Sung, on the other hand, loved foreign goods, especially clocks and foreign drinks of any kind.

The year 1910 was a memorable one in the East on account of the famous rubber boom. Like everybody else in Shanghai, whether Chinaman or foreigner, I had learnt to gamble on the Stock Exchange. I needed no capital; one had merely to walk into a stockbroker's office and place an order ahead. The shares were bought that day, but delivered on the settlement day in June or December. If they rose in the meanwhile and one cared to sell them, one could look forward to a fat cheque on settlement day without having put one's hand into one's pocket. That year every share connected with rubber shot up by leaps and bounds. Unfortunately, I never sold my shares to clear a large profit, and the inevitable crash soon came. Indeed, the close of my stay in

China was darkened by these worries, and I fell very ill with dysentery. Dr Krieg, the German doctor to whom I owe my life, insisted on my being taken to the General Hospital in order that I could be nursed better.

I spent many long weeks there in a large room, with Kwei Ching squatting on the verandah outside. An Oriental has but little sense of the passage of time, and Kwei Ching would remain all day within call of me without ever seeming bored. Ah Sung came occasionally too, but his was a more frivolous nature, and he soon went off again to enjoy himself in the city. Dr Krieg had insisted on my immediate return to Europe, and as I wished to see some of the cities of South China, I took a passage on the P & O *Somali*, which called at Foochow, Amoy, Swatow and Hong Kong.

There is always something sad about a departure, and I felt keenly the separation from Kwei Ching, who had been my constant companion and very faithful servant for more than two years, and from 'Gazelle eyes', the beautiful Ah Sung, to whose decorative presence I had grown more than accustomed. Both on their knees, with tears in their eyes and almost speechless with emotion, they implored me to take them with me to Europe. 'Let not the Shelter of the World cast away this slave like an old shoe! This dust-like one has sat in the shadow of his lord for many moons, and been blessed with the favour of the Glory of the East. The Consolation of his Ancestors must remember that he will have to cross many seas, and many lands, and each day as he awakens he will say, "Where is Kwei Ching?" And if Kwei Ching be not there to minister to his wants he will be as lost as a bird that has no wings.'

It required great courage to keep to my original intentions, but I foresaw so many storm-clouds ahead of me in Europe that I was unwilling to complicate matters further by arriving at the pension in Florence, at which my aunt was awaiting me, with a Chinese escort. Besides, I felt very sure that Kwei Ching would be most unhappy in Italy, or in England, and as I had no immediate intention of returning to China, it would be unfair to him to take him with me. Still, I will admit that when at last I boarded the *Somali*, when the last *adieux* had been made to Chinese and European friends, I felt more alone and friendless than I had ever felt before.

But the parting with Kwei Ching was not so final as I had antici-
pated. On the morning of the second day after leaving Shanghai we
reached the Pagoda anchorage, Foochow, and I was awakened by a
loud rasping sound, and by a series of cries. Then the boat heaved
slowly over to one side so that the wall of my cabin became the floor.
An English steward looked in to say we had run into a sandbank
while attempting to enter the harbour, and boats were being lowered.

I clambered up on deck as best I could, and was told that I
could take with me only what I could carry in my hands if I wanted
a place in one of the boats. I returned to my cabin and found Kwei
Ching, whom I thought I had left behind in Shanghai, systemati-
cally packing up my valuables in a small valise. In the East it is
useless to be surprised at anything. At any rate there was no time
for asking questions and, ten minutes later, I landed safely at
Foochow with Kwei Ching at my heels.

I spent a few days at Foochow and then went on to Amoy on a
Chinese steamer and finally reached Hong Kong. I spent a week
there and a few days at Macao.

I managed to persuade the faithful Kwei Ching to be reasonable.
He told me that the fortune-teller at the corner of the Siking Road
in Shanghai had foretold that I would be in danger, and Kwei
Ching had managed to slip on board at Woosung. Now that the
danger was over – for the fortune-teller had predicted only one –
Kwei Ching felt that I could be left to my own devices, especially
as he felt very much a fish out of water in Hong Kong, where Canto-
nese is spoken, and he could hardly make himself understood at all.

I presented Kwei Ching with two hundred dollars and all my
Chinese clothes, stipulating that the various fans, one embroidered
coat and one fur coat should be given to Ah Sung. This time it was
I who placed Kwei Ching upon a Shanghai-bound steamer. He
was not sorry to be returning to his city, but was still grieved to
leave me, in spite of my promise to come back very soon. 'Let not
the Protector of the Poor forget his servant,' said Kwei Ching at
parting, 'for this dust-like one will never stand in the shadow of a
new master, but will be waiting ready to salute the Spirit of Justice
when he returns to the Middle Kingdom.'

I have never seen Kwei Ching again. I heard, however, that for many years he went regularly to meet every mail steamer arriving from Europe, eagerly scrutinised the faces of the passengers, and that he became quite a familiar figure on the landing stage on the Bund and later perhaps a nuisance, for he disappeared from Shanghai altogether.

I always called China 'The land of the blue gown' because all servants and many shop-keepers just wore a blue gown over their usual Chinese dress. The significance of the buttons on the head caps of mandarins was very important and Li Hung Chang, the famous Chinese envoy so loyal to the Imperial Dynasty, was particularly concerned always about the right button to wear on his cap as various Imperial advancements were conferred upon him. Again, it must be remembered that when I was in China on this first occasion, pigtails were *de rigueur* and the Chinese servants spent hours combing, oiling and plaiting their pigtails. I was almost sorry, next time I visited China, to find that these unique adornments had disappeared for ever. Sir Robert Ho Tung, whom I knew well, always wore beautiful Chinese silk clothes, because he agreed with me in thinking Chinese costume not only more beautiful but also more healthy.

My great love for the country of my birth will never alter, although I am only too well aware that the present rulers do not represent the Chinese people – the most individualist race that I know. After I had written a book on South Africa, where I spent some nine months, I was invited by the government of Formosa to write a book about that wonderful island which, of course, is to me the real China of today. I would have been the guest of the government there while I wrote the book and if it proved satisfactory they would have been willing to buy a certain number of copies of the book. Unfortunately, owing to foreign currency shortage, they were not willing to pay the fare to Formosa and back, and as I found this might come to very nearly £1,000, I was not able to afford the journey – which has always been a great regret of mine. I would like, before I die, to have again a glimpse of the real and beautiful China which I know and love.

I learned many delightful customs in China: the intricacies of the tea and fan ceremonies, and to repeat the eternal cry of 'I am not worthy', which polite Chinese used on every occasion, especially when on a visit to a friend. On arrival, the visitor was expected to hurry towards the reception room, being mildly restrained all the time by the servants, who begged him to go very slowly – in China speed was considered a sign of humbleness and modesty, a leisurely gait a token of high birth. But all the delicate and beautiful manners of China could not excuse, in my heart, the treatment accorded the wretched coolies, whose lot the foreigners in China did nothing to ameliorate. By working to the very limit of his powers of endurance, a coolie earned just enough to keep body and soul together. For him there was no Sunday or holiday; for him no dole when out of work, no old-age pension. His chant, as he laboured, which has never changed for thousands of years – 'Oh-Ah-Hay. Hay-Ah-Oh' – haunts my ears today.

After I had first arrived in Shanghai in 1908 I used to frequent a small but lovely garden on the Bund which, in the hot weather, proved a sheer delight. I noticed, at first with surprise, a regulation written in English and Chinese on the gate: NO DOGS, NO CHINESE. I complained about this to several Shanghai friends, but they all said, 'Oh, don't trouble about that, you'll only get yourself unpopular.' Finally, I determined to put the matter to the test and as by this time, early 1909, I always wore Chinese dress, I drove in state in my own ricsha followed by two servants to the garden gate; immediately a Chinaman ran out and said in Chinese to me, 'Chinese are not admitted here'. I withered him with a glance and my servants said, 'This is an English resident'. The astonished Chinese gate-keeper went for assistance and a Sikh policeman then came and very politely said that if I were admitted, other Chinese would immediately want to enter the garden and he suggested I go away and put on European dress to avoid an incident. Of course I had my say – that I considered it outrageous that in a Chinese city, even if a Treaty Port, Chinamen should not be allowed into a garden in their own city. The incident was referred to in the local British press, which treated me simply as a harmless eccentric – which perhaps I really am.

Chapter Three

Memories of Imperial Russia

HAVING FINISHED WHAT I had to say about China, I naturally began
to think of Russia, because in 1933 I returned to Paris on the
Trans-Siberian railway on my way home from China.

Before that, however, all the year 1912 was spent by me in
Russia – a year of great happiness to me and one of the most
agreeable of my life. I have written about the Russia of 1912
already, but must touch again on a few of the more interesting
aspects of affairs there at that time – and a prelude to the appalling
murder of the Imperial Family very few years later.

I went to St Petersburg as my father's two sisters were brought
up at the Court of Hesse-Darmstadt and were contemporaries of
the Tsarina. My audience with the Imperial Family is still vivid
in my mind. I received a notice from the Court Chamberlain to
go to Tsarkoe Seloe, where the Court then was and where the
Emperor would receive me in audience on a certain day and at a
certain time. On the day appointed, one of the Court automobiles
fetched me and a few hours later I found myself within the
precincts of the palace, after passing innumerable sentries.

My first surprise was caused by the immense silence that reigned
in this royal palace; although the whole of the Imperial Family was
in residence, there seemed to be no bustle nor any movement at all.
There were sentries and Cossack attendants posted round the
large hall; but no one came or went. After waiting about an hour

in an ante-room I was conducted to the Chamberlain's apartment and taken immediately by His Excellency to a large studio, or morning room, with two bow windows. A few moments later a small door in the wall opened and the Emperor, dressed in a very simple Russian costume with tall boots, came into the room and greeted me with a grave, frank courtesy, to which I found it easy to respond. He spoke perfect English and seemed to be positively glad to talk in that language, telling me that the Empress and himself very often used it when alone together.

I was struck by the extraordinary melancholy of his eyes, which every now and then drooped as he spoke. The impression he conveyed was rather that of a country gentleman than of a monarch. As I sat talking to him I thought he must, to some extent, resemble Charles I of England and Louis XVI of France. All three were monarchs whose blameless and indeed edifying private lives stand out in strange relief amidst surroundings of incredible corruption and profligacy. All three were noble in thought and weak in action. All three fell under the fatal, if well-meant, influence of wives who had utterly failed to appreciate the mentality of their enemies and the dangers which lay ahead.

After I had chatted with the Emperor for about ten minutes he sent to enquire if the Empress had returned from a drive in the palace grounds. Shortly after, a lady-in-waiting came to us and asked the Emperor to come with me to the Empress's apartments.

I found the Tsarina very gracious and still retaining a certain soft Germanic beauty, but much stouter than the photographs of her would have led one to suppose. She remembered my father's two sisters very well and gaily related incidents of her schooldays in Darmstadt. As tea was being served in large glasses after the Russian fashion, the door was burst open and the Tsarevitch romped into the room. He had evidently expected to find his mother alone, and was very shy when he saw a strange visitor. A Scottish lady, his governess, and a tall Cossack accompanied him to the door and beckoned him back – but his mother told him to stay.

I have never seen a more timid child; though slightly built and boyishly dressed in a sailor suit, he looked far older than he really was. He had most extraordinarily gentle, almost beseeching eyes. After much hesitation and shyness on the part of the Tsarevitch, we finally became great friends, and he showed a lively interest in a little gold pencil-case which I carried; on being touched lightly at one end, out shot the pencil and, on being pressed a second time, the pencil withdrew into its shell. So delighted with the pencil was the boy that I laughingly asked the Empress to allow me to give it to him. The Empress hesitated a moment, but then thanked me and told her son to accept the pencil, which he did, making me a quaint little bow. I did not see any traces of ill-health on the Tsarevitch's features, but he was certainly a most nervous, timid lad.

The time came for me to return to St Petersburg, and it was with genuine gratitude that I thanked the Emperor and Empress for their kindness in receiving me so informally. The scene I left engraved itself extraordinarily clearly on my mind, and I can still see quite distinctly today the Empress seated on a sofa with the Tsarevitch beside her, his little arm round his mother's neck, the Grand Duchess Tatiana, a very beautiful girl, tall and slim and rather haughty, talking to the two ladies-in-waiting, as all three stood by the window; and the Tsar, also standing, lost, it seemed, in a reverie as he looked after me with those strangely wistful eyes.

The Tsarevitch suffered acutely from haemophilia and much controversy has been inspired by this illness and the influence that Rasputin gained over the Imperial Family thanks to the temporary cures which he was able to effect. I think we must, on that evidence, attribute Rasputin's influence to hypnotic powers, which he was able to exert even by telegram. Strange as this may seem, the solemn fact remains and cannot be gainsaid that not only did the Tsarevitch's health always improve when Rasputin was near him, but that the Tsarevitch actually depended upon Rasputin's ministrations to keep him alive. I cannot venture an explanation of how these alleviations of suffering were wrought, and Derevenko, physician in attendance on the Tsarevitch – not the sailor of the same name mentioned later – was frankly dumbfounded at Rasputin's successes.

Rasputin was born Gregory Efimovitch in 1871 in a small

Siberian village in the Province of Tobolsk. He came of peasant stock, but from an early age showed a marked difference of temperament from the peasants among whom he was brought up. He desired to enter the Church, received a religious education – by which I mean he learned the Catechism rather than the Three Rs – never mastered the art of writing correctly and was never admitted to Holy Orders. He adopted the mode of life of a *staretz* or wandering holy-man, such as Tolstoy describes in his *Childhood*. We do not have palmers in Europe any more but they would have been our nearest equivalent in the Latin West to the wanderers-for-God's-sake in Holy Russia.

Rasputin's peculiar powers of healing spread his fame as a wonder-worker. Whether these powers were miraculous, as was generally believed, or whether they derived from the peasant lore of a remote Siberia, we do not know, but in due course in Kazan he met the famous Bishop Michael and soon his name was heard even in St Petersburg. He travelled there modestly at the invitation of a religious organisation and made the acquaintance of Anna Alexandrovna Virubova, daughter of the Director of the Private Chancellery of His Majesty. Later I often met this lady, who was an intimate friend of the Tsarina and who succeeded in persuading her to allow Rasputin access to the afflicted Tsarevitch.

At that time, about 1908, this Prince had a Russian nurse, but was watched over by the sailor Derevenko, to whom he was devoted, and who never let his Imperial charge out of his sight. I cannot trace any rivalry between Derevenko and Rasputin. The sailor was so anxious for an amelioration in his charge's health that he was not in the least jealous when he found that, in very truth, Rasputin was able to effect an improvement.

It was the Countess Anna Virubova who was kind enough to take me to Rasputin's third-floor flat at 64 Gorokhovoy Street, in 1912. Rasputin held a kind of *levée* each morning and anybody who cared to call was made welcome. Unfortunately I did not speak Russian and could, therefore, do no more than just kiss his hand. Crowds of people were all around him. I saw rich ladies push bundles of notes into his hand; he never looked at the notes, but when he saw a poor supplicant merely handed on the money just as he had received it. He had no interest in money, though people asserted the contrary, since he had all he needed, as well as the protection and friendship of the entire Imperial Family.

My reason for wishing to see Rasputin was because at that time all St Petersburg was talking about his power of healing and how the Tsarevitch remained well, happy and healthy when Rasputin visited him daily.

Rasputin's power of healing was interesting and I had myself been present on a second occasion and was afforded the evidence of my own eyes. A mother called with her son who was epileptic and I saw him restore the child. What impressed me so much about his cure (which I was afterwards told was a permanent cure, not just relieving one epileptic fit) was that while he stroked the boy's head, muttering Russian prayers, breathing into his ears, mouth and nostrils, this huge, heavy peasant of a man seemed to become pale and even frail and when the boy was definitely cured (the whole affair lasted about ten minutes to a quarter of an hour) Rasputin sank back in a chair, utterly exhausted and almost helpless. It seemed indeed as if all the good had gone out of him. I considered it a great privilege to have seen undeniable proof of his extraordinary gift of healing. It may seem profane to mention Jesus Christ in any connection with Rasputin, but for all I know God may choose odd vessels to do his work.

The parrot cry against Rasputin that he was an unfrocked monk is utter nonsense since he had never taken Holy Orders, so could not have been an unfrocked monk. His immoral life had nothing to do with the powers of healing and prophecy which he undoubtedly possessed. The British like their heroes to be spotlessly white and their villains darkest black. They have tried to put Rasputin, who did so very much good in his lifetime, into the latter category. I shall always remember my two visits to him with gratitude and deep respect. He, for his part, did not care for English people at all and on my first visit he had received me somewhat cautiously, but the second time I was received with much greater enthusiasm, no doubt because the Countess Virubova had spoken favourably to him about me.

His gift of prophecy was well known too and referred to by the

Tsarina in her letters to the Tsar. There are many striking examples of this to be found in contemporary records, not by any means only those emanating from the closed circle of the Imperial Family. This prophetic gift embraced not only the fate of individuals but also the fate of the Empire; the outbreak of the 1914–18 war moved him to utterances every bit as biting and as doom-laden as those of the Prophet Jeremiah. He realised only too well that it would be the peasant class, from which he had sprung and with which he never lost contact, that would have to bear the brunt of the war. He realised that, after the events of the Russo-Japanese war and the Maxim Gorki Revolt, the Dynasty was not as firmly entrenched as it had been and feared, how rightly, the possibility of a revolution. In *The Secret Journal of Anna Virubova*, in the entry for 15 August 1915, we read:

> 'I can't give my blessing to this war,' said the Staretz. 'The country doesn't need it. The rich produce many children in their warm, comfortable houses, and room must be made for these children! And what's more, they want money and honours. War gives more opportunities to thieves than a bazaar! They can pinch all they want! That's why they have prepared the war with delight. They have need of it, whereas for Papa [the Tsar], it's nothing but a great danger!'
> And he continued:
> 'Papa got out of the Japanese War with nothing worse than a carbuncle, but this time it will be a wound that will never heal. The war is the enemy that is killing us all!'

This Journal has often been dismissed as spurious, but the vigorous expressions attributed to the *staretz* Rasputin encourage me to think that much of its content is genuine enough.

As Russian losses continued to mount, Rasputin's opposition to the war as contrary to the interests of the Russian people, the Russian Empire and the Russian Dynasty – contrary in fact to the Will of God for Holy Russia – earned him increasing unpopularity with the Allies, who suspected he might influence the Tsar to agree to a separate peace. It was said that he was in the pay of secretly pro-German bankers, that he and the Tsarina were in cabal to betray the Imperial Army. His murder by the combined efforts of Prince Yussopov and the Grand Duke Dmitri is a part of history on which I am reluctant to dwell. A commission of enquiry subsequently failed to substantiate any charge of corruption or treachery against this most enigmatic of men – though with all the officials and archives of the Empire at their disposal.

It is my view that, on the whole, his influence was rather good than bad, and had his advice been listened to, many subsequent evils would have been spared the world. It was Plato who said: 'All great natures have great vices as well as great virtues.'

In 1933 I returned to Paris, where I then lived, on the Trans-Siberian Railway. I was staying in Shanghai and met, by chance, the Soviet Ambassador to China, a very sociable gentleman; actually, we met in the Long Bar on the Bund, a famous resort in the Shanghai of those days, introduced by a famous journalist. At that time Russia was the only country that had its Embassy in Shanghai, the most important city in China. Nankin was the official capital where most of the foreign powers had their Embassies, though the British, if I remember right, continued to remain in Pekin at that time. I often went to Nankin and visited the big blue tomb of Sun Yat Sen. Anyhow – one day the Soviet Ambassador said that he had heard I was going back to Europe very soon and asked how I was travelling. I said I was going by sea to San Francisco, then by train across America and by sea to France. When he asked why didn't I choose the Trans-Siberian Railway, I replied that I had made enquiries and found that the fare (International Class) was about two hundred and fifty gold dollars from Vladivostok to Moscow, which was a great expense. He said he understood that, and I thought no more about the matter. However, one day the telephone in my room at the Cathay Hotel rang and someone from the Soviet Embassy asked if I could call round, as the Ambassador wanted to see me.

Very perplexed, as I have never troubled to hide my political opinions, I went to the Soviet Embassy and received via the Ambassador an invitation to return to Paris overland, as the guest of the Soviet authorities. I was very surprised and even a little flattered, as I knew I was of no importance. Anyhow, I was not rich enough to refuse such an extremely generous offer. I rushed round to the Japanese Consulate to get the necessary visa for the train via Mukden in Manchuria, which was then occupied by the Japanese. To my great surprise the Japanese authorities whom I had met socially greeted me with their usual smiles and told me they had heard I was to be the guest of the Soviet Government – and for that reason could not be issued with a visa. Finally I left Shanghai on a Norwegian cargo ship which had brought a large supply of timber from Russia to China and was returning to Vladivostok with a cargo of tea. Unfortunately the weather was very bad and I had a terrible six days journey on the Yellow Sea.

I was welcomed at Vladivostok and my troubles began the next day; I was being seen off at the station on the Trans-Siberian train, which at that time only left Vladivostok for Moscow three times a week; my luggage was put on the train and I was standing shaking hands with everybody when the train seemed to move out of the station – but I was reassured by my Russian friends that it was only manœuvring. After waiting a bit and seeing no sign of the train returning, we were informed that it had already started. Finally, I was put on to another train, which of course had no International Class, in the company of a Russian official. This train took me as far as Khabarovsk. I waited there until another Trans-Siberian train picked me up, but again cruel fate had not sounded the all-clear in my favour.

After two or three days in the train there was a railway accident and I was precipitated through the window of my carriage on to a Russian steppe in the middle of an October night. My great fear was that fire would break out, as I could not move from where I was. Finally, however, some Red Guards on the train managed to pull the passengers out through the window. It transpired that only the International Class coach, which was the last one on the train, had overturned as the couplings had broken. After this there were no more accidents or incidents and I reached Moscow whole and safe.

I now want to speak about the train journey across Siberia. There were apparently three classes on this express – International Class, Soft Class and Hard Class, which we in our bourgeois way would no doubt have called 1st, 2nd and 3rd, but in Russia there was only one class and this was subdivided as I have stated. I was treated with every conceivable kindness. My passport had been taken from me at Vladivostok and locked up because the Russians at that time were terrified of thieves stealing foreign passports. All gold objects such as cufflinks, watches, etc., had to be declared in Vladivostok at the outset of the journey, but these were not taken away from me. The food on the train was really excellent – but then I have never had an opportunity before, and fear I never shall again, of having caviar three times a day. Crushed caviar was served, but to my taste it was just as good as the more usual grey Beluga eggs. I was supplied with delicious Georgian wines and was beginning to feel mellow and most grateful to the Soviet Union when we arrived at Sverdlovsk, formerly called Ekatarineburg, where the train stopped for about five or six hours. This town was where the Imperial Family had been murdered. Many of the travellers on the train went to visit the villa where this tragedy happened, but I could not bring myself to do so, and remained in the train.

I was particularly grateful to the Russians I met that they never attempted to explain the wonders and advantages of their political system – this was perhaps because they knew too well my opinions, though this again made me so surprised that they should take the trouble to invite me to make this unforgettable journey. I fear they must have thought I was a more important author than I am and that once I had seen how smoothly everything worked, I would write a favourable book – but I do not know if this was their intention, as I was never asked to do so. I very much fear I was no use to the Soviet authorities, as I never wrote anything about it until now. Naturally, no-one is more in disagreement with the whole idea of communism than I am, but I must say that the high level of their artistic achievements is cause for much congratulation.

It was when we got to Moscow that for the first time in my life I met André Gide. This was just before he wrote his book *Retour à l'URSS* criticising the Soviet Union, which hitherto he had praised. Before I left Moscow, where I spent about ten days, I was taken almost every evening to the Bolshoi Theatre, where the ballet and opera were of the same high level as they had been when I was last in the same theatre in 1912. In fact, I remember the Imperial box with the double eagle still stood in the theatre – filled of course by factory workers and other employed persons whose turn it was to visit the ballet. I remember that in '33 Ulanova was beginning her wonderful career as a dancer. I did sometimes meet Russians speaking French or German – usually German – who did not hesitate to give me their reasons why they objected to the Soviet regime. I remember on one occasion going to a Turkish bath (or should I say Russian bath?) in Moscow. The masseur, not knowing I was a guest of the government, thinking I was just an ordinary British tourist, poured forth his woes with great emphasis and lack of reticence. As I love an argument, I soon found myself defending the Soviet conditions with an energy I have never since felt tempted to repeat. While he soaped and massaged me we became good friends and I was forgiven for contradicting him. Decidedly – *tout savonner c'est tout pardonner*.

To illustrate the generosity of the Soviet Government, I was issued with a ticket not as far, as I expected, as just to the Russo-Polish frontier, but all the way to Paris – as was André Gide. I got to know him very well on the journey to Paris, as we stopped off in Warsaw for twenty-four hours – he to see Polish friends and I to visit restaurants I had known before.

Chapter Four

Mr Norris

I AM VERY glad that Christopher Isherwood and I met in the early 'thirties because he made me the hero or villain of his best seller *Mr Norris Changes Trains* and I feel happy that I was able to render him this service, simply by existing and providing him with so much successful material that after the publication of that book he became such a well-known author.

When Isherwood wrote *Mr Norris Changes Trains* everybody assumed I was the actual Mr Norris. On this account I wrote an article for *Punch* which I entitled *The Importance of not being Norris* and which saw the light of day in that paper on 17 November 1954. I may perhaps be permitted to quote from this article:

> The rumour that I am the Mr Norris who changed trains has again been given currency, this time in an article by Claud Cockburn.
> I do not know how the rumour got around. Christopher Isherwood always said that it was a composite character, and although many of my *obiter dicta* were put into the mouth of Mr Norris, I must once and for all decline to admit any closer resemblance, much as I admire the enchanting hero of so successful a novel. The rumour started when I lived in the same pension as Isherwood did in pre-Hitler Berlin, a pension which hardly resembled the caricature of it and its landlady portrayed in *I am a Camera*. Also, before it was ever published, Isherwood sent me a

37

typescript of the novel for my comments and approval. *Voilà tout*.

A great many years ago, when I was a slip of a boy of only fifty and knew no better, I published my autobiography. The blurb was written by Isherwood, which ended with the paragraph:

'His strange and frequently secret missions read as thrillingly as the pages of an Oppenheim. Gerald Hamilton is candid and never shameless; we follow him into strange places and forgive him much. . . .'

All these facts no doubt point to my being a Norris-like eccentric. Indeed, G. W. Stonier, reviewing my autobiography, said of me:

'He is an Irishman, a Radical, a weather cock, a bit of a crank. Most of his time has been spent travelling from one continent to another, negotiating with ambassadors and starting movements. . . . He was a Sinn Feiner in Ireland, a Royalist in Greece.'

The point is that between the publication of my book and today so much more Norris-like things have happened to me that, were I to write a sequel, I might only confirm the Norris legend rather than destroy it. Once at a New Year's Eve party held, I forget why, in Brussels of all places, the poet Wystan Auden, who was present, wrote a long poem devoting one verse to each guest at the party. The one that concerned myself was:

> Uncle Gerald, your charm is a mystery
> I shall not attempt to define.
> It concerns your appearance, your history
> Your knowledge of footmen and wine.
> So it's you that I now raise my cup to,
> Though I haven't the faintest idea
> What the hell it is you are up to
> But I wish you a happy New Year.

The importance of not being Norris is manifest, but the importance of resembling him in a few things is also great. I did indeed make a bid for peace during the last war, but it was not, as Mr Cockburn suggests, 'under the ægis of the Papal Nuncio or the Spanish Embassy'. There is, in fact, no Papal Nuncio in England, only an Apostolic Delegate. If it was under the ægis of anybody it was under that of the late Duke of Bedford. And as to trying to reach Ireland disguised as a nun, my plan was thwarted and I was

38

arrested before I had even got my coif in place. Herbert Morrison signed a *lettre de cachet* and confined me in the local Bastille, Brixton, for daring to meddle in high politics. My stay was not protracted and I was not charged with any offence, so that I feel I have but little right to wear the Old Brixton tie.

Another Norris-like occasion which I remember concerns an occasion a few years back when, being very hard up, it occurred to me that I might be able to raise funds on one or other of the few decorations which former monarchs had been misguided enough to confer upon me. Reluctant to go myself on so delicate a mission, I asked my cook, who had to go out shopping, to do the deed for me, and I entrusted her with a somewhat showy plaque to take to the pawnbroker's and suggested she might get a fiver or a tenner loan on it. She fished it out of her shopping basket from among the potatoes and the cauliflower and laid it on the counter. The astonished pawnbroker, on hearing to whom it belonged, rang me up and asked what sum I required. I said boldly a tenner, but he said 'Oh we can let you have that or more, if you like'. It was only then that I realised, what I had never known before, that my decoration was made of pure gold and real stones and was not, as I had always thought, imitation. I rushed to my cupboard and extracted my remaining ornaments which went the same way, where they remained until at a later date I recovered them all, only to sell them outright to a dealer in decorations at Charing Cross. The late Tsar Ferdinand of Bulgaria, whose guest I was twice at Sofia when he was on the throne, and a third time at Coburg for the so-called Coburg wedding in October 1932, had been good enough to confer several decorations on me, for no other reason that I can think of than the fact that they contributed considerably to the embellishment of what might otherwise be considered a too un-Courtly appearance.

A columnist writing about me in 1946 said, 'Gerald Hamilton, writer and traveller, is shortly off to Lisbon, which cynical people would take as meaning that a revolution is imminent in that country. . . . His passion in life is good food, and his dinner parties at his studio house at Chelsea are famous. He spends most of his time preparing for them.'

To my surprise, this paragraph was headed 'The Last Gentleman'.

What with revolutions, the cuisine, and literary work, I have always managed to keep the 'pot boiling', unlike poor Mr Norris, who was pursued to the uttermost ends of the earth by a peripatetic secretary, an official whom the writer of these lines has never been fortunate enough to possess.

Christopher Isherwood himself, in the preface to my book *Mr Norris & I*, says in the first paragraph, 'Now and then I am asked if the character of Mr Norris in my novel (called *Mr Norris Changes Trains* in England and *The Last of Mr Norris* in America) is based on my old friend Gerald Hamilton. Sometimes I answer "No" to this question, sometimes "Yes" – according to my mood and the suspected motives of the questioner. Neither answer is more than partially true.'

I am ready to admit, however, that there is much of me in the character of Mr Norris (not, I hasten to say, in the sex life of that worthy), in his manner of speech, his reluctance to face the issue, these would fit a description of me at that very distant Berlin period. Christopher and I visited the high spots of Berlin night life, giggled a lot and attempted to enjoy ourselves on our very limited means.

One visitor of ours during that Berlin period which certainly must not be omitted from this story was Guy Burgess. Much later, when he was front-page news, I pretended to have discovered a letter from Mr Norris to Christopher Isherwood, which I published in *The Spectator* on 4th November 1955.

My dear Christopher
    I have much to thank you for no doubt. Who indeed, would have heard of Arthur Norris had you not written a best-seller about him? And although, together, of course, with that charming Miss Bowles (with whom, I regret to say, I have altogether lost touch), I may justly claim to have had no small share in the foundations of your fortunes, this letter is in no way intended as a reproach. I merely wish to draw your attention to one of those amusing discrepancies between fact and fiction, the piquancy of which has been underlined by recent events.
    'In the novel you insisted, in your humorous way, that it was I who had introduced you, all unwilling, to a master-spy. In fact, of course, the only real – or (should I say) really successful – spy

whom I ever met was introduced to me by you in, of course, the best faith.

Do you remember the time you first introduced me to Guy Burgess? I do. It was in Brussels, which was our next stop after Berlin – not South America to which you exiled me in the novel. Burgess, then in his middle twenties, was showing signs of the dissipation for which he afterwards became notorious. Stephen Spender, with those ever-lofty standards of his, was already openly disapproving. You, and Wystan Auden, were rather more tolerant, if I remember right.

Though dissipated, however, Burgess was never violent; he could drink the whole night through without becoming aggressive. I remember one Sunday morning he turned up, very early indeed, at the villa which I occupied at Uccle, looking, even for him, peculiarly grubby and dishevelled; he told me, so I understood, that he had just come from Mass. I remarked that I was surprised and delighted to hear it. After talking at cross purposes for some time, I realised that he was referring not to Holy Mass but to Maas, a singularly louche night haunt near the Gare du Nord in Brussels.

Soon after, when I was paying one of my then infrequent visits to London, Guy Burgess invited me to luncheon with him at the Reform Club. He received me with his usual hearty aplomb, but as we sat drinking sherry in the somewhat overwhelming grandeur of the entrance hall, his spirits seemed to take a sudden downward turn. 'This club depresses me terribly sometimes,' he said, 'there are no page boys. Have you ever noticed that, Arthur?' 'Come, come, dear boy,' I said, 'you mustn't crab your own club. Try to enjoy such solid mid-Victorian amenities as it does provide. Take another sip of this excellent Waterloo sherry.'

At luncheon, our conversation turned to Soviet Russia, which I was then proposing to visit on my way home from Shanghai, where I was bound as a member of an international humanitarian delegation. (This you must remember, Christopher, was during my regenerate, fellow-travelling period, before my final conversion to the sacred cause of Absolutism.) Burgess was positively naive in his envy of my good fortune in being able to visit the Communist holy land, the Mecca of the proletariat. He was most eager that we should meet as soon as I returned, so that he could share my impressions.

The details of my journey – it was a veritable global tour – have little relevance. In Moscow, where I stayed for a few days only, I met André Gide and travelled back with him as far as Paris. He was openly voicing dissatisfaction with the Soviet paradise which he afterwards expressed in print in *Retour à l'URSS*. Later, in London, at a second luncheon with Guy Burgess at the Reform, I myself felt compelled to say in all sincerity that I had not been so favourably impressed as I had hoped to be by our Russian comrades and their *milieu*. I half expected an outburst of indignation and was most surprised, I remember, by Guy Burgess's seeming indifference, particularly when I went on to stress the prevailing intolerance of the Soviet regime towards certain modes of behaviour, tendencies, tastes, aberrations – call them what you will – which both he and André Gide had in common. I thought at the time that I was witnessing one of those little triumphs of political zeal over personal predilection. Little did I realise that I was in the presence of a professional paid agent, an *âme damnée* of the Kremlin!

Came the war, so long feared and awaited, yet so utterly unlike anything any of us had expected. While you, my dear Christopher, were far away, meditating in California, your poor friend Arthur Norris – ever, no matter what the apparent changes in his ideological allegiances, a sincere friend of Peace – found himself (for the second time) a detainee under the iniquitously repressing regulation, 18B. I refer, of course, to my attempt – unsuccessful but praiseworthy, I think you will admit – to bring about a cessation of hostilities via the intervention of His Holiness. . . .

It was not until some years after peace had actually been signed that I again encountered Guy Burgess. He was now a professional *diplomate de carrière*. We bumped into each other in the Christmas rush at Fortnum's. Guy had a tin under his arm. I said 'Caviare, I suppose?' – but it turned out to be Elvas plums. We agreed to meet for dinner.

The evening developed along markedly saturnalian lines. Guy was accompanied by a friend who enjoys, among many major claims to fame, the distinction – one which I, naturally, appreciate – of having sat for the portraits of some of the most popular characters in the fiction of our time. He may not be the only begetter of 'Miles Malpractice', 'Ambrose Silk' and 'Anthony Blanche', but he is at any rate, the only one worth knowing. I will call him, for the purposes of this letter, Mr Q.

Guy Burgess had lost none of his tastes for the lower night haunts. After dinner he and Q guided me to a basement club in Soho so manifestly louche that it reminded me, with, I confess, a slight pang of nostalgia, of the closing hours of the Weimar Republic, which you, dear Christopher, have so brilliantly portrayed. While we were there, the place was raided. The police approached our table. Q, who was by this time very drunk indeed, on being asked for his name and address, gave his name, and added: 'I live in Mayfair. No doubt you come from some dreary suburb.' I remarked to Guy Burgess that, in my experience, this was a most tactless way of receiving the attentions of the civil arm. Guy, however, for his part, behaved with such assured nonchalance, giving his own name, address, and occupation, in stentorian tones, that I could only conclude that a new – and how welcome! – spirit of tolerance was prevailing in Whitehall.

A few days later we met in another club, the respectable kind; no less respectable, indeed, though rather more modest, than the Reform or the Athenaeum. There was an unfortunate scene when the elated Q insisted on tweaking the nose of a distinguished cleric who was sipping a cocktail in the billiard room. 'Oh!' he cried, in the grips of one of those strange fits of idealism which, as you may have noticed, beset the most unlikely subjects, 'so you're one of those jolly, hail-fellow-well-met padres, are you, my dear?' He was immediately requested to leave, and to take his guests with him. A gallant suggestion by Guy Burgess that we should all adjourn to the Traveller's was vetoed by myself as inviting too much hubris for any one day.

The very last time I saw Guy Burgess was a week or so before his final disappearance. I need hardly tell you, my dear Christopher, that I had no notion whatsoever of his real intentions, else I should not have hesitated to take steps to – shall I say – sublate, if not indeed actively to frustrate them. We met in yet another of those nachtlokals to which we both – though, as I now begin to suspect, for rather different reasons – seem to have been so addicted. Burgess remarked: 'Surely Arthur, you're much too old now to wear a wig!' To which I exclaimed: 'My dear boy! It is septuagenarian stubble!'

Soon after, the inexorable machine of international politics swept him away. With all – and I am fully conscious of what is meant by all – his faults, I cannot help regarding his memory, at any rate, with a certain affection. I often wish he and Fräulein Schroeder could have met. She would, I am sure, have called him 'Herr Doktor' almost at once.

> Believe me, dear boy,
> Your ancient, and indeed, I might say,
> almost indestructible friend,
> ARTHUR NORRIS.

While on the subject of Guy Burgess, I must remark on one point in his favour: it seems to me that he never attempted to hide his extreme affection for everything to do with Soviet Russia.

But let us leave Guy Burgess and return to Christopher Isherwood, who has now been a friend of mine for nearly forty years. When I lived in Berlin we met almost daily after our first meeting under the auspices of Alesteir Crowley. Oddly enough it was not true, as Christopher wrote in *Mr Norris Changes Trains*, that I ever lived in the famous pension immortalised by him. But I was a frequent visitor there. I always remember my first meeting with Jean Ross, who in Christopher's Berlin stories became the famous Sally Bowles. I met her one evening and we became instant friends. She asked me to call the next morning and I said I would do so and take her to lunch. She of course lived in the famous pension. When I called with my usual punctuality exactly at twelve o'clock, I was told that Miss Ross was in her bath. However a gay voice rang out down the passage – 'Is that you, Gerald? Come and talk to me, darling, while I'm having my bath.' I have often maintained that I am the last of the Puritans, but have never found anybody yet to believe me. I felt rather startled at this warm invitation to sit in the bathroom while a lady I had only met the night before was performing her ablutions. However, I went into the bathroom and thanks to the steaming bath and to the nauseating smell of bath oil, I managed to escape and waited for Miss Ross in the sitting-room, where I was regaled by the chatter of 'Fräulein Schneider' the landlady.

Christopher came with us to lunch and he was in great form, earning his livelihood at the time by teaching English to various pupils. My memories of him are today very vivid. At that time he was very gay and always ready to laugh. Today he has changed and every time I have seen him during the last year or two here in London he strikes me as being much more austere and serious than he used to be. He dressed in the usual casual style of a student of the time, but was always particularly neat and the favourite tenant of 'Fräulein Schneider'. We generally met for lunch at a pension where for a very small sum an excellent meal was provided. Amongst those who occasionally came to this table was Beatrix Lehmann, who was not then as famous as she was later to become. Her brother John Lehmann also often came to Germany to visit us. I think Claud Cockburn also honoured this pension with his somewhat untidy presence.

After we all left Berlin, Christopher and I met in Brussels and both took lodgings there. I remember E M Forster coming to visit Christopher at Ostend one summer when we were there for a few weeks. Morgan Forster is undoubtedly a genius and before I met him I had of course read *Passage to India*. In Ostend I remember he enjoyed playing the somewhat untuned piano in the pension, which he said was better than nothing. I remember Benjamin Britten coming to visit Christopher in Brussels, and Stephen Spender as well as W H Auden often came over. Both of these poets I had already met in Berlin and it is odd now to look back on how all these people have become very famous. Does fame always spoil people's character? I think it well may do, but I have remained friends of the people I have mentioned for many years now – though I have not seen as much of them as I would like to have done.

Chapter Five

Winston Churchill

IT WAS IN the summer of 1913 that I took a small villa a few miles from Dieppe at a place called Puy. Living at Dieppe at that time was a very distinguished English lady, Lady Blanche Hozier, to whom I was introduced by a Belgian friend, the Baronne de Vaughan, who was the morganatic widow of King Leopold II of the Belgians (his second wife), and who was in Dieppe that summer. Lady Blanche occupied a very charming house and was looked after by a very capable lady; Mrs Scott was, I think, her name. In the first few days of my stay near Dieppe I often called to see Lady Blanche, who, by this time I had realised, was the late Sir Winston Churchill's mother-in-law. At that time he was at the Admiralty, and one day there came a telegram to say that he was coming to visit his mother-in-law in the Admiralty yacht *Enchantress*. Great preparations were made for his brief stay and one day Mrs Scott was sent in the afternoon to get the right sort of brandy to put in this distinguished politician's bedroom and the whole town seemed anxious to welcome Winston Churchill.

I did not meet him on this occasion and I never met either of Lady Blanche's daughters – Mrs Romilly being Lady Churchill's sister.

I knew both of Mrs Romilly's sons – Giles and the other one, Esmond, who was an ardent Red, fought in Spain later on the side of the Republicans and was killed in the Second World War. He married one of the Freeman-Mitford girls, Jessica.

It was, I knew, hard not to admire Winston Churchill, but somehow or other I never really succeeded in doing so. I admired him very much as a wonderful writer, a great orator and a gifted painter, but politically I felt him to be temperamentally unbalanced.

When the *lettre de cachet* during the Second World War which ordered my internment, though signed by the Home Secretary, Herbert Morrison, was, I learned after, at the request of the Prime Minister, Sir Winston Churchill, I determined to get even with him. A wonderful opportunity occurred when the great sculptor Oscar Nemon was commissioned to do a statue of Sir Winston for the Guildhall. It so happened that my weight and measurements at that time were the same as Churchill's and as the great leader only had time to have his face sculpted, a Russian lady friend proposed to Mr Nemon that I should sit for the statue. This I did. I both liked and admired Oscar Nemon very much; he may have very contra feelings about myself!!

The statue was duly unveiled at the Guildhall and the usual flow of politic speeches were delivered. I sat quiet through the ceremony and it was only after it was all over that I called a press conference and announced that I, an ex 18B detainee, had sat for the statue, which was more of me than of Winston Churchill. A terrible storm broke over my bald head, as can be expected, and it was some days before it all died down. In order to avoid the press, I retired into the wilds of Notting Hill Gate, where I hid myself. I have heard various accounts of what this great war leader had to say about this instance, the least offensive being 'Could they not have found someone else?' Hardly had this mild scandal died down – it was after all nothing but a prank which it had amused me to play – when I found myself again in troubled waters over the late Sir Winston Churchill.

When I was in South Africa, sent there by the publishers to write my book *Jacaranda*, I visited a house in Pretoria where Churchill lodged when, as a British officer, he had been taken prisoner by the Boers. I was assured by the Government officials there that he had been allowed complete liberty to go where he wanted in the town of Pretoria, having been given his parole. Later, as is well known, he blacked his face and managed to escape to

Lourenço Marques and finally reach England. In my book I did in fact say that he had broken his parole, but apparently his version was that he never gave his parole. At any rate I found myself the subject of another storm and threatened with legal proceedings for libel. I remained calm, but not so my publishers. Fortunately Sir Winston's secretary, Mr Anthony Montague Brown, arranged that copies of the book should be recalled and a small printed paragraph inserted saying that the author had been mistaken. I also had to write a letter of abject apology, which was graciously accepted, and to Sir Winston's eternal credit it must be said that if not forgiven, I was at least treated in a generous spirit for which I am very grateful. Friends of mine kept saying 'When are you going to leave poor Churchill alone?' and one well-known peer said at a dinner party, 'Gerald insulted poor Churchill over the matter of his statue at the Guildhall and then libels him in his book. I am sure he can find some way when the old man dies to disorganise his funeral.'

Fortunately, this did not happen and indeed my respect for him, such as it is, would never have permitted me to do other than pray for him. I have my own feelings, but I did regard him as a war-monger and indeed still do. His courage during the war was a great example to everybody – but need the war ever have happened? It seems always to be forgotten that it was the British who declared war on Germany and I firmly believe that negotiations could have prevented this war. Churchill himself said on a famous occasion: 'Better jaw, jaw than war, war'.

Churchill's political attitude during the war shocked and appalled me, particularly at the Yalta Conference when Poland was handed, so to speak, on a silver platter to the Russian criminals and, after being photographed with Roosevelt and Stalin, Churchill came back to tell the Commons that he had every confidence in the capability of his friend Marshal Stalin. The betrayal of Poland, a country the British public were told they went to war to defend, was one of the most disgraceful acts for which Churchill was partly responsible. If it was not so tragic it would be humorous to remember the terrible Katyn Massacres when eleven thousand Polish officers were massacred by the Russians and then at the Nuremberg trials the Russians succeeded in pretending that the

Germans had murdered these officers and one of the indictments against the German defendants was this fact. When it is remembered that Russian judges sat on the bench with their Allied colleagues, I can only repeat that if the whole thing was not so tragic it would be simply farcical.

At the time I did what I could to draw attention to this outrage. The *Catholic Herald* of 18 October 1946 was the first newspaper that consented to publish my comments after I had read the full text of the Nuremberg judgment. I pointed out that the atrocious murders in Lidice and Oradour were referred to at great length and the perpetrators of these outrages duly castigated. I looked in vain, however, for any mention of the more appalling massacre at Katyn of these Polish officers, who by this time had been proved to have been murdered by the Russians. I did not leave off drawing attention to this matter and the *Daily Telegraph* of 26 August 1954 allowed me to return to the attack and under the heading of 'Outdoing the Nazis' the editor published a conclusive letter, which ended: 'The cold-blooded murder of the brave Polish officers at Katyn by the Russians alone exceeded in horror anything the Germans ever did or were accused of doing.' Finally, in view of the publication by Lord Russell of Liverpool of a recent book, the editor of the *Daily Telegraph* published in his issue of 24 November 1956 a further protest from me. From this letter I quote a brief paragraph: 'On the indictment the Germans were accused of the atrocious Katyn murders. Today it has been proved conclusively that the real murderers were the Russians, who, however, were allowed to sit in judgment in Nuremberg on the Germans, although their Government was guilty of one of the many crimes attributed to the defeated.'

But nobody seems to care very much about this or about anything in connection with the last war. In the meantime the Poles in England, who fought with the Allies so bravely, managed to live somehow or other without receiving the ample grants from the British Government which they certainly deserved.

However, a play called *Soldiers* running in London at the time of writing suggests a possibility of Churchill wishing to get rid of the Polish General Sikorski. The reason for this was that he was frightened that the General would bedevil his relations with Stalin. This was because it had come to Churchill's knowledge that the large number of Polish officers murdered by the Russians was also known to General Sikorski, who was anxious for a Red Cross mission to be allowed to disinter the bodies and prove to the world that the Russians were the murderers, not the Germans. The General was so insistent on this point that Churchill had every reason to wish to be rid of him. Personally, I cannot possibly bring myself to believe that Churchill was a party to a plot to sabotage the aeroplane in which the General was flying to London. People who do not agree with me instantly quote Churchill's contempt for human life when he authorised Bomber Harris to destroy German cities such as Dresden and that he would, therefore, hardly stop at the life of one man who was in his way. The Jesuit side of Churchill's character often obtruded itself and he always believed that the end justified the means.

Anyhow, the truth will probably never be known and perhaps it is better it should not be. I personally was closely connected with the Polish Government in Exile stationed in London – a friend not only of the Ambassador but of most of his staff. I was favoured with a seat for the Requiem Mass at Westminster Cathedral for General Sikorski only a row behind the seats of the British Cabinet, the Polish Cabinet being in front. I was very favourably impressed to notice that at the moment of the Elevation, Churchill knelt and buried his head in his hands – while Eden, loyal no doubt to his masonic oaths as a Freemason who had joined one of the Ulster Lodges, sat upright staring straight in front of him.

Let me end this criticism of the late Sir Winston Churchill on a happier note. I have always said that a son of his great father, Lord Randolph, ought indeed to have been a Cabinet Minister earlier than was the case, not because I feel that his influence and policies would have been excellent ones, but because he came from a family whose traditions and whose members devoted themselves to the government of their country and of course they came from noble stock. I have always said that if I have to be governed, I would rather be governed by middle-class people such as myself, or by my social superiors, rather than by my social inferiors as is the case today.

Chapter Six

Maundy Gregory and Others

I BECAME A close friend of the late Maundy Gregory in the twenties and was originally introduced to him by A J A Symons. The latter's connection with Maundy Gregory was due to the fact that he possessed most of the Corvo manuscripts in existence and Maundy Gregory was a great admirer of Fr Rolfe, or Baron Corvo, as he liked to call himself. He bought all the MSS he could afford at a very high price. Symons took me to see him, thinking we could be useful to one another. I liked Maundy Gregory and I know the feeling was reciprocated. At this time, Maundy Gregory was the greatest, perhaps the only, 'Title Broker' in England. He undoubtedly managed to secure baronetcies and peerages for his clients and his earnings at this time must have been enormous.

I had no interest in these English titles and decorations. My job was to help to secure for his clients foreign ones. One particular foreign decoration was the Order of Christ of Portugal, because this Order could be worn with a bright red ribbon which most people mistook for the French Legion of Honour. Any expenses incurred while travelling were generously reimbursed by Maundy Gregory, who I remember asking what I would require a day; on hearing me say 'Oh, about £10', he answered 'Oh, you would probably require more than that – probably not less than £15 a day.'

When my second autobiography came out in 1956, I was taken

to task by one distinguished reviewer for not mentioning my connection with Maundy Gregory. The reason for this was because I well knew that many of his successful clients were still alive and it would cause only sorrow in families to know that the head of the family had not been decorated as a real hero. As people were angry with me for not referring to this matter, I inserted a letter in the *Spectator* of 23 November 1956, explaining my position. It may be remembered that Maundy Gregory, after many years of prosperity, came to grief finally over one of his few failures – a naval officer who had the boldness to sue him. As can be well imagined, most people were shy of doing this for fear of the ridicule attached. Maundy Gregory was, if my memory serves me, sentenced to three months' imprisonment. He went to live in Paris on his release from prison and was there when Paris was occupied by the Germans. He died in a Paris hospital during the war.

I have often been asked to describe Maundy Gregory – how he spoke, what he wore – even what he liked to eat. Actually, when I was out with him he would have seemed to a bystander to have been a very ordinary 'City gent'. He always wore black or dark suits and he had a taxi which he had bought, explaining to me that the reason for doing so was because it was easier in such a vehicle to move in and out of London traffic than it would have been in a large car. He was very well known in most London restaurants of good repute, but such meals as I had with him were usually taken at the 'Ambassadeurs' close to the Mayfair Hotel. One had to be a member of this Club to entertain at it. One thing I did notice about Gregory which commanded my respect was that I never knew him to be drunk, although no one loved good wines and old brandy more than he did. His choice of food at a luncheon or dinner party showed that he was a real connoisseur of food, if not a gourmet. With regard to conversation, Maundy Gregory was very well informed about all political eventualities and naturally had a great many friends who were Members of Parliament and members of the House of Lords. He had, not surprisingly, a great hatred of any form of Socialism, a sentiment I readily shared.

It was thanks to my introduction that Maundy Gregory met King George of Greece, then in exile in London, and it was after lunching with this King and myself that he returned home to the charming lady whom he always introduced as his wife; she was then ill and he persuaded her to write out her Will on the back of a menu card which he had in his pocket after this lunch party. She signed the Will and it was witnessed by two servants. She died in their Thames-side home but suspicions were aroused that she might have been poisoned and an order for the exhumation of the body was granted at the request of her relatives. When the body was exhumed it was found that it had been buried in the grounds of their house close to the river and was, therefore, water-sodden. Any traces which there might have been of arsenic or any other poison which it was thought might have been administered had, therefore, disappeared. All thoughts of prosecution were naturally dropped. I myself do not know whether there were any grounds for suspicion, but I could never imagine kind, jovial Maundy Gregory committing a murder, especially the murder of his wife, of whom he was particularly fond.

Maundy Gregory never opened his files for me to see, so I do not know who bought their titles and who earned them, though I have very shrewd notions. One case I do know of was Sir George Watson, the Maypole Dairy millionaire, who bought a baronetcy through Maundy Gregory. He left two sons, one of them, Peter Watson, was a close friend of mine. He it was who financed the wartime magazine *Horizon*, so admirably edited by Cyril Connolly. Peter Watson was a famous collector of art, paintings, etc, and possessed some wonderful Picassos. He used to live in Paris in the Rue du Bac, but came to live in England when war broke out and had a flat in Palace Gate. He then moved into a magnificent new flat in Rutland Gate, where he died in his bath. This must have been in 1955. He himself did not care for titles at all, but was a kind of young Maecenas. His death was a tremendous loss to all his many friends.

With regard to the moral side of Maundy Gregory's activities, I honestly do not see why people should hold up their hands in horror at his successful manipulation of genuine titles. A rich man can always buy a valuable picture; why should he not buy a title? In his day, before the Second World War, titles had a great glamour that has completely gone today when prize fighters, cricketers, seamen, and actors among others are admitted to the House of Lords.

Maundy Gregory was the son, if I remember right, of a Southampton clergyman, but he had a great dislike for this Hampshire town and to him, as he often repeated, England was simply London and nowhere else really appealed to him. His Whitehall offices were specially rigged up to impress callers who might become clients and he pretended, even to me, to have a private line communicating with the Prime Minister. People genuinely anxious to buy a title would apparently swallow any kind of elaborate staging that would seem suspicious to most other people.

The Baron de Forest, who had been a great friend of Edward VII and a Member of Parliament for a short time, and who later took the name of Count de Bendern living mostly in Zürich and having become a subject of Liechtenstein, was a friend of Maundy Gregory. Whether Maundy Gregory helped the very rich Baron in his affairs and change of nationality, I do not know. But I do remember once going to a political meeting of the Baron de Forest's, whose English at that time was not quite perfect. He was standing as a candidate for Parliament and a left-wing member of the audience called out 'Why are you a Baron?' De Forest replied, 'I am Baron because my father was.' The heckler shouted back, 'Well, I wish to God your mother had been!'

Count Arnold de Bendern, as he had become, died very recently in Biarritz, aged 89, and was one of the most astonishing characters I have ever met. What I remember chiefly about him when I last saw him in Zürich was his love of great cleanliness. This implied that he would never touch a bank note that had been in circulation – and he had other similar foibles. He was the adopted son of Baron Hirsch and acquired the title of Count de Bendern when he relinquished his citizenship of Great Britain in 1932 and became a naturalised citizen of Liechtenstein. Later on he declared: 'I have always been an advanced Radical and have remained one. I have also remained a convinced pacifist.' His friends all knew him as

54

'Tootie' – a less appropriate name I could hardly conceive, because he set great value on an extreme dignity and observance of the rules of protocol. The Count was last in the news when his Franz Hals picture 'The Flute Player' – one of the best of Hals's paintings and valued at about a quarter of a million pounds – was stolen. It had been deposited in a Geneva bank, but when the wrappings were removed it was discovered that a worthless object had been substituted for the Franz Hals. Finally the painting was recovered from a left-luggage locker by the police. All this happened only in 1967. The Count expressed his gratitude to the Government of Liechtenstein, which had always given him every assistance, by the gift on his death of ten paintings valued at several hundred thousand pounds.

I never met either of the Count's two sons, the elder of whom had quarrelled with his father whom he had not seen for some ten years before the latter's death. The younger, however, is a well-known figure in London society.

I was for a time a close friend of Alesteir Crowley and, for some months after giving up my flat in Berlin, a paying guest at his apartment there. Much has been written about Crowley, especially by the gifted author John Symonds, who has written two books on this 'Master of Magic'. The first time I ever met him was in fact in Berlin long before I moved into his apartment. It was really the idea of Christopher Isherwood for us to call upon him, as Crowley had at that time an exhibition of his weird paintings in a Berlin gallery. We telephoned and called to see him and both came away delighted at having met this wicked man and thrilled at the welcome he gave us. I often called to see him during the following years and it must have been in '31 that I moved into his apartment.

With regard to Crowley's magic, he had indeed many followers and admirers, but I myself was never a firm believer either in his capacity to perform successful magic rites or in his own honest belief in the power of these attempts. Obviously it paid him well to continue and he received allowances and gifts from many female believers in his magic.

At the time of his Berlin residence his lady friend was a Frau Busch. She was known as the 'Red Angel'. One of her great attractions as far as I was concerned was her skill in the kitchen. She was indeed a wonderful cook and one of those instinctive ones who, without following the recipe, knows at once how much of this or that to put into the casserole or soup.

Quarrels broke out consistently between them and these sometimes ended up disastrously. Here I am perhaps to be permitted to quote from John Symonds's book entitled *The Great Beast*, published in 1951, about what happened one evening when I returned home about midnight.

> . . . and found Trudy lying stark naked on the floor, apparently asleep. It was winter and the fire had burnt out. Feeling that she had lost her way, Hamilton shook the dozing Beast.
>
> 'Is Trudy ill?' he asked.
>
> 'What, hasn't that bitch gone to bed yet?'
>
> Crowley tumbled off the bed (he was half dressed and still had his shoes on) and gave poor Scarlet Woman the biggest kick he, Hamilton, had ever witnessed.
>
> The flat was strewn with broken crockery: plate-throwing being one of Trudy's means of defence. Trudy sprang up and a struggle then commenced. Crowley reached out for some rope which was kept handy.
>
> 'Help me bind her!' he roared at Hamilton. 'Don't stand there looking like a bloody gentleman!'
>
> Hamilton tactfully retreated towards the door, ignoring cries for help from both Scarlet Woman and Master Therion. Then, judiciously, he called the doctor, who soon arrived, prepared his hypodermic syringe and in a business-like fashion administered a much-needed narcotic to poor Trudy.

John Symonds goes on to refer to the gift of £50 given to Crowley by the British Government to report on my activities in Berlin. I naturally never knew of this until after Crowley's death, when his literary executor and another close friend gave me proof. What is piquant in this matter is that on one of my journeys to London, Gerald Yorke asked me to take some English money back to Berlin and to give it to Crowley. This I did. The amount entrusted to me was the very £50 in cash that my host had earned by writing a report upon my very harmless activities.

Before I ever knew him, Crowley had lived in Paris until he was expelled from there by the French authorities, and then in Cefalu in Sicily where strange rites had been alleged in some temple he had built there in his villa. The libel case he brought against Nina Hamnet at the beginning of the war was of course a godsend to the evening papers. Nina in her book *Naked Torso* had accused Crowley of sacrificing a cat in the temple at Cefalu and of lots of other horrible practices. Whether he ever did such a thing, I do not know – I rather doubt it. He lost the libel case and I think was made bankrupt after that. It would be pointless for me to go into the details and success or failure of his magic powers. As I knew him he was really a '*bon bourgeois*' with a great fondness for good talk and good food. His one delight was to play endless games of chess with worthy opponents and after the last war had broken out he ensconced himself in a little flat in Jermyn Street where some of the best chess players in England forgathered.

My recollections of Crowley in London at this time, after the Second World War had broken out, was of our meals together in the Grill Room of the Piccadilly Hotel, which was conveniently close to his flat in Jermyn Street. Walking with Crowley to the hotel, whenever he saw a Roman Catholic priest in the street he performed some strange rite and muttered incantations bringing down a curse on the devoted head of the unfortunate priest. He loathed the Roman Catholic Church and I enquired how he could distinguish so quickly which were Church of England clergy and which RC, but he said he could do so easily. He never cursed the C of E clergy because he said they were not real clergy, which I interpreted as some kind of tacit recognition of the Roman Catholic Church being the real Church of Christ.

Crowley's arrival in the Grill Room of the Piccadilly was always announced by his advent being preceded by a strong odour of ether. Later, the smell of brandy predominated. He always seemed able to consume unlimited quantities of the strongest alcohol without this having any effect upon him. Maurice Richardson refers to this in some of his writings – notably in the

57

epilogue he was kind enough to write for my book *Mr Norris and I*.

When I arrived in London at the beginning of the war, I took a flat in Hanover Square and Crowley obtained one in the same block, just under mine. At that time I was a practising Catholic and on Easter Day 1940 or 1941 went down the staircase early in the morning, passing Crowley's door which was wide open as he had asthma trouble; he shouted out, 'Where are you going?' I said, 'I'm going to Mass at St James's, Spanish Place, and as it's Easter I'm taking communion.' He shouted back, 'Well, I hope your god will taste nice, you're such a bloody gourmet.'

I was so happy when, in 1921, I finally obtained an apartment in Paris in the Avenue du Colonel Bonnet in the 16th *arrondissement*, and this gave me an opportunity of enjoying life and trying to be useful to those ideals which I cherished. The household was small, but I was able to have two servants – a cook and a manservant, both with old-fashioned and even feudal ideas – and I, who was shocked by people whose servants answered the telephone brusquely and to my mind rudely, therefore made my small staff, when they lifted the receiver, enquire '*à qui ai-je l'honneur?*'. American friends especially chaffed me over this reply to their calls.

It was in Paris then that I first met Cocteau, whom I saw for the last time when he was in Oxford a few years ago. I used to meet him frequently at the *Bœuf sur le Toit*, where he was to be found most evenings in the company of his particular friend, a most conspicuous and handsome young man called Radriguet. On the sudden death of this young man, Cocteau was disconsolate and sat alone always on the point of tears. I ventured to suggest to Herbert Jacob, who was managing the *Bœuf sur le Toit* at the time, that the establishment should be called, in view of Cocteau's loss, '*Le Veuf sur le Toit*' – a piece of humour which was much quoted at the time by others who claimed to have said it first, but I still insist on my copyright to the remark!!

I might also refer to a visit Lord Alfred Douglas paid to me in

Paris. We had been friends since long before the First World War and I believe I was the only fairly close friend of his who never once quarrelled with him. I sympathised very much when he had to go to prison for libelling Winston Churchill. I think he was a fearless, obstinate but lovable character. Of course I never met Oscar Wilde who died when I was twelve, but my friendship with Alfred Douglas lasted until his death. I used to go to Brighton to visit him very often, and also saw his mother, on several occasions and his sister. At that time they all lived in the same house. Later he moved to a small flat and was almost dependent on an allowance given him by the late Chips Channon, who often told me about Bosie's gratitude and the happy talks they had had together. After his mother's conversion to the Catholic Church, Douglas followed suit and was indeed the most intransigent of Catholics that I have ever met. I sincerely hope that he is now in heaven and, if so, may have re-met the spirit of Oscar Wilde, another Catholic convert.

Chapter Seven

Roger Casement

I FIRST MET Roger Casement at the house of Mrs Alice Green (a woman devotedly dedicated to the cause of Irish Nationalism), in London about 1912, when Casement had not long been back from Putamayo, and his report of the atrocities there was still a subject of conversation in London, where he was considered to be a great hero. It was at this time that Casement talked of his hopes for Irish independence. It is interesting to remember now that he was always against John Redmond and the latter's idea of Home Rule. Casement wished for a complete severance of political ties between the two countries, but on an amicable, economic and reasonable basis.

Casement was indeed something of a prophet, because, unlike most people in the year 1913, he considered war with Germany to be inevitable, and it was then he decided that Ireland's interests would be best advanced by an alliance with Germany. When war broke out I had decided to go to Spain, a country I have always loved and which I guessed would remain neutral.

I feel I must here give some account of the Irish troubles just before the First World War. The Ulster leaders, suffering as always from a violent attack of Ulsterics, were opposing the Liberal Government's desires for a Home Rule settlement. Home Rule, they said, meant Rome Rule. There were threats of mutiny at the

Curragh and the whole of Ireland was seething with discontent and anxiety. Carson being an Irishman and born in Dublin had every right to express his views, unpalatable though they were to Casement and his friends, but why 'Galloper' Smith, as he was called, should go over from Liverpool to excite the Ulster leaders, I have never understood. He was not an Irishman and, as far as I know, could claim no Irish blood, but it was his policy at that time to fish in troubled waters, hoping to turn this to his political advantage. Later, of course, he became the first Lord Birkenhead and was Attorney General prosecuting Roger Casement at the Old Bailey.

It is not necessary for me to go into all the details of the Irish position at this time. Unfortunately, Casement often seemed to me to be very simple politically. He never seemed to realise that his very famous report about the Congo atrocities, for which he was granted his knighthood, was utilised by the British Government, not because the latter cared one way or the other about the fate of the wretched black population, exploited to get rubber, but because they wanted to discredit the Belgian Government which had, in the words of Casement's great friend, author of *Red Rubber*, E D Morell, 'got there first'.

After the Congo, Casement was sent to Peru to write a report for the Government on the conditions in Putamayo. Mr René McColl wrote a very fair book about Casement called *Roger Casement – a New Judgment*, published by Hamish Hamilton in 1956. In this book he goes into great detail about both the Congo and Peruvian reports.

When the First World War broke out, Casement felt it was his duty to go to America and visit the Irish political associations there to decide whether or not Ireland should throw in its lot with Germany. Later, Casement decided to take the risk of going to Germany and he sailed from New York on the Norwegian ship *Oskar II*. This ship was duly intercepted by HMS *Hibernia*, but Casement was not recognised, nor was he looked for. Indeed most of the passengers, who were mainly Germans, thought this mysterious 'Mr Landy' was a British spy.

It may be remembered that in Oslo (then Christiania) the British Ambassador there tried by various means to have Casement kidnapped or assassinated. However, Casement reached Berlin in safety. As it was, I was destined never to see Casement again, nor was I allowed to leave England until after the war when I had been released from internment.

I would here like to give a few personal recollections of this Irish hero. He was what the French would call an *'enjôleur'*, a word hard to translate, but one might say a charmer. I remember his habit particularly of stroking his well-trimmed beard as he was speaking, and his way of staring at his interlocutor when addressing him – always directly facing him. He was very socially inclined, liked to go to parties; he was rather tight where money was concerned, frequently elaborately entering his out-of-pocket expenses – even such minor ones as bus fares – into a small notebook that he carried. He was in fact the opposite of extravagant. I have seen him smoke, but would not describe him as a smoker and I believe he gave it up when he went to America. He had very distinct artistic leanings and enjoyed going to picture galleries; he also enjoyed haranguing those who accompanied him on the beauty or lack of beauty of the pictures we were looking at. Although an Irish revolutionary, he really seemed to be an ideal English gentleman, well educated, courteous and admirable in any social gathering. It still seems to be incredible that this man, whose sincerity was never in doubt, and who was responsible for saving so many lives in the Congo and Peru, could have aroused such violent hatred in England. But his soft voice and smiling eyes endeared him to many of his supporters. Less, however, to those with whom he had to deal in Berlin. He was convinced, and nothing would alter this opinion of his, that with a victory for Germany the Irish Republic would be set up as an ally of Germany and to this end he worked in that country. He addressed the Irish prisoners of war taken by the Germans and tried, without much success, to induce them to join the Irish battalion that he wished to form as part of the Imperial German Army.

Finally, before leaving Germany it seemed to him that Germany would not be able to send troops to Ireland. All they could, and did, send was Casement in a 'U' boat to Tralee and a shipload of arms on the *Aud*, a ship commanded by Captain Spindler. Captain Spindler, whom I was able to meet in Berlin after the First World War, confirmed this, and it was Casement's intention to do what he could to prevent the Rising taking place. René McColl admits that this was probably true. In a letter published in the *New Statesman* on 21 April 1956 he says: 'Mr Gerald Hamilton raises the interesting point as to the motivation which finally led Casement to go to Ireland in a "U" boat just before the Dublin Rising of Easter 1916. He feels that neither your able reviewer, Mr Ralph Partridge, nor I have sufficiently stressed that the real reason for this forlorn hope of a journey was that Casement, far from wishing to take part in the Rising, wanted at all costs to stop it, since he was then convinced that it would fail.'

Before leaving the subject of René McColl's book, I want to congratulate Mr Partridge on his detailed essay 'A Target for Prejudice'; also on his skill in stressing the fact, so little appreciated, that because 'Casement practised homosexuality he was, by implication, hanged for doing so, just as much as for his so-called treachery'. I, who was by this time in London, hoped for a reprieve. Indeed, agitation for this was gaining momentum every day. The White House and the Vatican were even in touch over a concerted effort to ask King George to show mercy to his prisoner. However, the sinister figures of Admiral Hall and Sir Basil Thomson, moving rapidly behind the scenes, were determined not to be baulked of their prey so easily. They immediately circulated photostats and typescripts of the Diaries which they alleged to be Casement's. These reached the eyes of everybody of importance who hoped for a reprieve; those, for instance, of the American Ambassador and the Spanish Ambassador and Cardinal Bourne. In Mr Partridge's own words, 'Even allowing for the exacerbation of ignoble feelings in war, our Government's behaviour was blaggardly, to use Sergeant Sullivan's old-fashioned language.'

Mr Montgomery Hyde is the great authority on the trial and conviction of Roger Casement. It must never be forgotten, he says, that it was not Casement and the Irish Nationalists who first committed what the English called 'treason', but the Ulster leaders like

Carson and F E Smith, who organised the gun-running for their armed forces and who clearly defied the British Government by saying that, if the Home Rule Bill were passed, they would resist its implementation by force of arms, and it is ironic to remember that at Casement's trial, F E Smith, who by that time had become Attorney General and later Lord Birkenhead, was the most ferocious enemy of the Irishman in the dock. Under the heading 'Two Cases of Treason', the well-known barrister R Barry O'Brien wrote a long article in the *Daily Telegraph* of 9 August 1957, most of which was taken up with the Casement trial. Sir F E Smith, when application was made to him for leave to appeal to the Lords, refused his fiat, although in the trial of William Joyce Sir Hartley Shawcross, then Attorney General, granted the fiat.

The Casement trial was the first known occasion on which a formal judgment had been given by a court on the meaning of the Treason Act of 1351, in relation to the crime of adhering to the King's enemies.

Written in Norman French without any punctuation, the relevant section of the six-centuries-old statute appeared to be capable of several meanings and nearly two of the four days of the trial were spent in discussing it. The defence contended that the statute limited the crime to adhering within the realm. It argued that as Casement had been charged with adhering to the King's enemies elsewhere than in the realm – in Germany – no offence was disclosed.

The court held that the statute covered the offence of adhering both within and without the realm, and a motion to quash the indictment failed. Casement was found guilty and sentenced to death. His appeal was dismissed by the Court of Criminal Appeal after a further two-day discussion on the point of law and the defence applied to Sir F E Smith for leave to appeal to the House of Lords.

The late Professor J H Morgan, KC, and another member of the defence team, Thomas Artemus Jones, went to see the Attorney General. Smith told them that their point was trivial and refused to give his certificate. 'Trivial' seemed a surprising comment, particularly as the Lord Chief Justice, Lord Reading, who presided

64

at the trial, had said in his judgment on the motion to quash the indictment that the point merited careful examination by the court.

Mr Barry O'Brien wrote:

> That night, 19th July, 1916, Morgan wrote to Smith in an attempt to persuade him to reconsider his decision. I found a copy of this letter while going through Morgan's papers as his literary executor. He wrote: 'As a constitutional lawyer whose word is supposed to carry some weight in such matters and who necessarily is cautious in committing himself, I am of the opinion that the point of law is anything but trivial and your argument against us anything but conclusive.
>
> 'More than that I have discussed the point with two legal scholars whose reputation in this country stands higher than that of any other lawyer in such matters (one was Professor William Holdsworth) and they were clearly of the opinion that the matter was one of great doubt and considerable perplexity.'
>
> Smith did not reply to the letter. And he did not change his decision. Casement was hanged on August 3rd.

In 1966, as I had never seen the ceremony of 'Trooping the Colour', I watched it on television out of curiosity. I was amused to see the Queen of England leading her Irish Guards back to her palace to the strains of the splendid music of 'The Wearing of the Green', as I remembered the words of this inspiring march – one of the lines runs, 'The red on England's cruel flag is the blood of Irishmen'.

It is strange to think that before half a century had elapsed after Casement's death, his remains were accorded a State Funeral and the British Ambassador to the Irish Republic stood to attention before the bier. Casement, who had been a Protestant, registered at Pentonville Prison as a Roman Catholic, in order to be near Irish fellow countrymen and a Catholic priest. His conversion to the Roman Catholic Church followed, and he received his first communion according to the rites of that Church on the day of his execution. The prison chaplain who accompanied him to the scaffold, Father Thomas Carey, was approached, after the execution, by an Irish lady who wished to assure him that she would pray for Roger Casement. The chaplain said to her, briefly, 'Madam, do not pray for him, pray to him, for he is surely now in Paradise'.

On the 50th anniversary of Casement's execution I was asked by the Editor of the *Labour Monthly* to write an article about him. I did this and it was published in the August issue, 1966.

A strange pendant to this story is the fact that, after my arrest and after being bullied by Sir Basil Thomson, who said to me: 'You are sitting in the chair your friend Casement recently sat in and you know what is going to happen to him, don't you, well I expect the same fate now awaits you', I had some measure of revenge. I was allowed a passport on my release from internment to go to Switzerland for medical treatment. I did not get further than Paris, where I had many friends, both Ministers and officials, who gave me every help and encouragement to stay there. I was slightly amused one day to read in the English papers of the arrest of Sir Basil Thomson, who had been caught in Hyde Park with a young girl. He drew the constable who had arrested him aside and said he was the Commissioner of Police. The constable, not believing him, said, 'I don't care if you are the Negus of Abyssinia, you are coming with me.' Later, when it was too late to withdraw the charge, Sir Basil Thomson appeared before the Magistrate, who remarked that the publicity in the newspapers was enough punishment by itself. Sir Basil left England at once and by a great coincidence when I was calling on somebody at the St Lazare Hotel I found myself going up in the lift with no less a person than the unsavoury Sir Basil. The lift was one of those old-fashioned cage-like French lifts that move very slowly. I immediately turned on Sir Basil and never in my life have I been so abusive to any human being as I was on this occasion. He kept trying to stop the lift, but, in the end, the lift went to the top floor. I thoroughly enjoyed myself that morning, I must admit.

I wrote about this incident in the *New Statesman* on 3 December 1955. It happened that the late Gilbert Harding, at the time of publication of this article, was in a hospital in the Brompton Road, and though I did not at that time know Gilbert, he wrote to

66

congratulate me on what I had written. As he was interested in the personality of Roger Casement, I called to see him and saw quite a lot of him later in Brighton. On Gilbert Harding's death, I was invited to write a chapter of a book which was a collection of reminiscences of his friends, which I did. The book appeared in 1961.

At the Paris Peace Conference just after the First World War, there was an unofficial Irish Delegation headed by Sean T O'Kelly, later to become President of the Irish Republic, and my old friend George Gavan-Duffy, who had been Casement's solicitor. I have explained how I got my passport returned to me for a journey to Switzerland, but stopped in Paris, where I was made welcome by many French and cosmopolitan friends. These two Irish gentlemen had been informed from Dublin that I was expected and I saw them daily. I met various interesting people at the Irish Delegation's quarters at the Grand Hotel, including Prince Aziz Hassan of Egypt, later to play an important role in my life.

In Paris at the same time was Monsignor Ceretti, later Cardinal, who represented the Vatican's interests officially at the Peace Conference. He was a friend of mine whom I met when I was in Rome at the beginning of the First World War. The two heads of the Irish Delegation very much wanted to meet this Monsignor and I was able to arrange this and took them to the flat occupied at the time by Mgr Ceretti. They were thus able to put the case for Irish complete independence and for the establishment of a Republic, which was carefully transmitted to Rome and approved by Cardinal Gaspari, the Vatican Secretary of State, whom I knew. I sat in the same room, but aloof from the long conversation, as I did not want to interfere; but from the gratitude expressed to me by Sean T O'Kelly and George Gavan-Duffy I almost thought I had done something very clever indeed, which was hardly the case.

Later in Paris, I had the great privilege and honour of meeting for the first time President de Valera and the Countess Markievicz, who paid a visit to Paris and stayed with the Delegation at the Grand Hotel. President de Valera was an impressive figure at the time, tall, aloof, unsmiling, but in the eyes of every Irishman a unique hero. His innumerable escapes from British jails were a saga in themselves. The Countess, on the other hand, a hard but most attractive woman, was born with the sacred flame of patriotic ardour. It may be remembered that she was sentenced to death by the British after the 1916 revolution, a sentence later commuted to life imprisonment at Aylesbury jail. She was, however, released and was thus able to accompany the President to Paris early in 1919.

Sean T O'Kelly, or I should say President O'Kelly, was a character in himself. He was on every British black list, but managed to travel on a passport, borrowed from his brother, on which the photograph resembled him closely. Gavan-Duffy on the other hand had not, so far as I know, had any obstacles put in his path to prevent him being in Paris. O'Kelly's wife, an erudite lady, spoke perfect Gaelic and was good enough to give me a few lessons in my own language, also to write my name in Irish, and in my youthful enthusiasm I opened an account in a Paris bank, insisting on signing my cheques in Irish, much to the annoyance and confusion, I fear, of the French cashiers.

Recent events, at the time of writing, in Northern Ireland naturally remind me of my youth, as I was brought up in County Tyrone, and said on one occasion that if there's one thing that history never does it is to repeat itself. Nevertheless, this is precisely what has happened in Ireland. From the time of my childhood when Carson and 'Galloper' Smith decided on armed resistance to the passing of the Home Rule Bill ('Home Rule means Rome Rule!') until today when the fortunes of Northern Ireland seem to have fallen into the hands of unscrupulous rabble rousers like the Reverend Paisley, Ireland has known no real peace.

My quarrel with the Northern Ireland leaders is their affection for, almost deification of, the Usurper of Orange who forced that atrocious drink gin down the throats of British citizens that had hitherto been accustomed to good ale or French wines. The Usurper had two minions, Keppel and Bentinck, to whom he gave the monopoly of the gin trade and who incidentally made immense fortunes out of this. True, later came the Gin Riots in

George II's reign and the numerous deaths that were thus caused when the King wished to levy a trifling tax on the sale of gin.

I have always found Ulster people utterly unrealistic with regard to this Usurper and in my young days I often attended dinners when the most important toast was to 'The little gentleman in black velvet' – namely the mole that constructed the molehill on which the Usurper's horse tripped and threw the rider to his death.

In Northern Ireland they still do not take into consideration the irregular life of the Usurper who was a homosexual surrounded by his good-looking minions and in a recent paper-back by James Graham a chapter is devoted to this topic, proving – not that there has ever been any doubt about the matter – that the Usurper was a dissolute homosexual. He speaks well of the loyalty of William's young friend Keppel and when William died in April 1702, probably of tuberculosis, and was lying in state, Graham says: 'Keppel was not there, but Bentinck stood beside him rigid and stolid in his mourning cloak, dull, reliable and wooden. He was doing his duty, as he had always done.'

An amusing quotation from this book is this: 'After King Edward [Edward VII] died, Mrs Keppel, his famous mistress, then a sprightly old lady, was asked about her relationship with Edward. "Of course I went to bed with him," she is supposed to have said, "and it wasn't the first time a Keppel was in a King's bed." '

Lastly, it must also be remembered that the Battle of the Boyne was won by the Usurper thanks to the courage and prowess of his Hessian mercenaries who defeated the real King's British and French troops.

An aspiring young courtier at the court of Charles II was one John Churchill who tried his best to win over the Duke of York to be his patron. Finally, he managed to introduce his sister, Arabella Churchill, into the future King's bed. She bore the future King a son who was the first Duke of Berwick. Colonel John Churchill was promoted to be Colonel in Charge of the King's Guards and had various other honours conferred upon him. When, however, William of Orange threatened to invade England, he sent an enormous amount of money in gold to Colonel Churchill to win him over and there was a historic meeting between Colonel Churchill and Lord Arlington, who enquired 'and what is in your pockets, dear Colonel, oranges or candle grease?'. The Colonel had to confess that oranges were in his pocket. Of course, he betrayed his King by refusing to lead the Royal Guards from Hounslow, where they were stationed, to London to defend the King. A sad story, but a typical one of the times.

It may not be realised the Colonel Churchill was in a few years, in the reign of Queen Anne, to become the public hero, the first Duke of Marlborough.

A few years ago I went to Ireland with Brian Desmond Hurst, the well-known film director, who was directing the last filming of *Playboy of the Western World* with Siobhan McKenna starring in it. I am always glad of an excuse to return to Ireland, but in the small village of Inch in County Kerry the weather was very bad and I soon fell ill. My kind host took me back from the location to the cottage I was living in and the sympathetic lady who owned the cottage put me to bed and, finding I had a temperature, suddenly said: 'Now would you be a Catholic or a Protestant?' I assured her I had been baptised as a Roman Catholic. She then gave a sigh of relief and said: 'Glory be – you understand, it would be awkward to have a dead Protestant lying about in the village!' The lady was very charming and devout and told me that her son, who was at Maynooth College, would be home soon and 'Can you believe it?' she said, 'has already learned to speak the grand Latin'.

I am glad to say that the film was a great success, but it always bores me to watch a film being shot because when the director cries out 'Action!' one finds that the same scene has to be re-acted several times before it is considered perfect. However, my love of the play helped to stifle my feelings of boredom.

Chapter Eight

The Duke of Bedford's Peace Move

I WAS IN close touch with the late Duke of Bedford during the last war, being, as I have always been, opposed to all wars and, most especially, to the last World War. Actually, before war broke out, I harkened to the various slogans, such as 'Mosley for Peace', but never joined his movement as I am against the use of force in political argument. The Duke of Bedford, a much more placid man and a man determined to do what he could to bring peace about, impressed me from the outset very favourably. I was fortunately able to establish connection with the Vatican through a neutral Embassy. I visited the Duke where he was then living at Newton Stewart in Wigtownshire, and it was finally decided that I should go to Ireland to continue negotiations which had begun quite favourably. However, the exit permit to Ireland was refused me and, after some hesitation, I was invited to join a party of Irish nuns from a convent near London. The Reverend Mother was, as she explained, used to the 'troubles' in our country and one nun, who was in weak health, was ready to yield her place to me. Suitable attire was found for me in the convent and it was felt that a party of six nuns, prayer books and rosaries in hand, would not be interfered with.

There exists an amusing picture by Ronald Searle of me in nun's costume about to embark for Ireland. Unfortunately, thanks, I suppose, to the venality of a decoding clerk in the neutral Embassy which had been so helpful to me, my plan was betrayed and so I never reached Ireland on that occasion. What happened afterwards has been variously described in the press. I was, of course, arrested, and after being held for nearly a week *incommunicado* at Scotland Yard, finding that I could not be prosecuted on any particular account, an order was served on me under Clause 18B of the Defence of the Realm Act committing me to Brixton Prison. I was immediately put in a wing occupied by other interned persons, all of whom were held there, like myself, without charge or trial. It was there that I met Sir Oswald Mosley, Captain Ramsay, the Tory MP for Perth, Admiral Sir Barry Domvile, and many other charming people. We internees had our cell doors open in the morning and they were not closed until we went to bed at night. We could, of course, have our own food and furniture. Many amusing incidents took place and the second day after my arrival Mosley's mother called to see him and the warder called out to the top landing, 'Mosley, come down, there's a visitor for you.' Many of the interned people shouted out at the wretched warder, 'Call him Sir Oswald, you bastard!'

I should here perhaps refer to the terms of the suggested peace treaty which had reached the Germans through Baron Weisacker, their Ambassador at the Vatican. It was stipulated that the British Empire should remain intact. This was very important as it showed that neither the Duke nor myself was acting in an anti-British capacity. All we wanted was peace and to save lives. Had we been successful, not only would this have happened, but Russia would certainly not have been in the powerful position she is in today and a greater danger to our civilisation than ever the German Nazis were. We both thought that the Germans would sooner or later get rid of Hitler themselves, as they very nearly did at the time of the July plot, and, above all, the persecution of Jews and similar cruelties could have been stopped. It is here interesting to read the wording of the *lettre de cachet* which is contained in James Graham-Murray's *The Sword and the Umbrella*, published by Anthony Gibbs & Phillips in 1964.

The detention order sets out that it was made 'because the Secretary of State had reasonable cause to believe the said Gerald

Bernard Francis Hamilton to have been recently concerned in the preparation of acts prejudicial to the public safety or the defence of the realm and that by reason thereof it was necessary to exercise control over him'.

It goes on to give particulars of these acts:

'1. having been refused an exit permit [he] endeavoured to make arrangements to leave this country illegally in order to go to Eire with the intention of communicating with the Vatican or alternatively of proceeding via Spain to the Vatican in the hope and with the object that, being opposed to the war, he might endeavour to promote peace on terms favourable to the enemy;
and

'2. had indicated that if he succeeded in getting to Eire he would go to the German Legation in Dublin where he expected he would be sympathetically received.'

Though the order was made out at the end of July it was not executed until the end of August 1941, when Mr Hamilton was arrested at his home in Glebe Place, Chelsea, and lodged in Brixton prison.

Some four months later, at the beginning of 1942, he was released under Regulation 18a and allowed home. For the remainder of the war he was treated as an enemy alien and had to report to the police periodically and so on.

Mr Graham-Murray ended his account about me in his book, which shows that he must have had access to the Home Office archives, with this paragraph:

He had been complaining (to the Intelligence Officer who interrogated him) that since he was neither a Fascist nor a Communist, he could not understand why he had been interned. 'I don't know what you are politically,' said the man from MI5, 'but I do know you're a damn nuisance.'

In fact, I remember this being said to me.

Mr Graham-Murray quotes me as describing the genesis of my 'peace move' as follows:

As the war progressed I discussed the situation with my great friend, the late Mgr Barton-Brown, whom I first met in Rome many years ago, when he was attached to the Vatican. We both came to the same conclusion, that a continuation of the war would put the Soviet Government in a commanding position and that, if the Allies won, the Tyrant Hitler might disappear, but a worse Tyrant, Stalin, would be there instead.

The casualties and loss of life and the possibility that the war might continue indefinitely, impressed us very much and we wondered what could be done.

Mgr Barton-Brown wrote to Mgr Montini (the present Pope) who was working in the Vatican and whom he knew well, but the answer he received was unhelpful, so I decided to approach my friend, Cardinal Maglione.

I found it quite impossible to conduct my correspondence with Cardinal Maglione through the ordinary channels, and requested and received permission from a neutral Embassy to use the facilities of this Embassy for my communications.

The late Duke of Bedford was very enthusiastic about my attempts to establish contact with a view to a possible peace. The Duke of Bedford was in touch with the late Dr Bell, Bishop of Chichester at that time, and a meeting was arranged between the three of us.

I was asked by Cardinal Maglione to suggest terms for the possible meeting between diplomats to negotiate an eventual armistice. Mgr Barton-Brown and I finally drafted a long document, which was approved and sent to the Cardinal, to be shown to the German Ambassador to the Vatican.

In his book, James Graham-Murray continued:

Quite what Mr Hamilton and Mgr Barton-Brown hoped to achieve with their document, which was sent via the neutral Embassy bag from London and intercepted by the British authorities, is hard to see. The timing of it could scarcely have been more ill-chosen, an aspect which the Vatican – the most delicate and well-informed sounding board in Europe – would have noticed at once.

The German invasion of Russia was in full swing and going according to plan, and this 'peace move' it must be borne in mind was in no way concerned with the German Opposition, it was to be an approach to the Nazi Government who were then at their most belligerent.

Mr Hamilton, as we have seen, had already tried to get to Eire before embarking on the 'peace' operation. The Duke of Bedford (then the Marquis of Tavistock) had already been to Dublin early in 1940 with the purpose and result indicated in telegrams exchanged between the Minister in Dublin and the Foreign Ministry in Berlin.

A group was formed called the Home Office Advisory Committee and each detainee was interviewed by members of this Committee. I must have given a good impression, because it was decided to order my release. I was not represented by any lawyer, but made my own little speech, claiming, as a Roman Catholic, that I had every right to appeal to the Vatican and make a visit *ad limina*. All I wanted was to bring about peace, which surely was not a criminal intention and no one could accuse me of being either a fascist or a communist. I here now give the text of the order which set me free:

Home Office
Whitehall
2nd January 1942

862746
Sir,
I am directed by the Secretary of State to inform you that he has considered your case again in the light of the report received from the Advisory Committee and has decided to revoke the Order for your detention under Regulation 18B of the Defence (General) Regulations, 1939, and has made an order under Regulation 18A. A copy of this Order has been handed to you.

I am, Sir,
Your obedient Servant
(signed)
J L DE LA COUR.

G B F Hamilton, Esq,
c/o The Governor,
Brixton Prison.

Soon after my release from Brixton jail, Sir Oswald Mosley, whom I knew as Tom Mosley as did all his friends, was transferred to Holloway jail where his wife Diana was confined, so that husband and wife could be together, as the war seemed to be pursuing a course which would take many years to run.

As I had become a close friend of Mosley when we were interned at Brixton, he wanted to see me in Holloway and for me to meet Lady Mosley whom I had not then met. He obtained permission for a visiting permit to be sent to me which gave my name and stated that I was entitled to visit 'MOSLEY O & D'. This caused me much merriment and I suppose the spread of socialism in England was unwilling to give the two internees their proper names: Sir Oswald Mosley, BT and The Honourable Lady Mosley – as indeed the visiting permit should have been worded.

The Duke of Bedford himself was not interfered with, but Herbert Morrison, the then Home Secretary, kept assuring Parliament that he had his eye on this recalcitrant Duke. The truth is, of course, that, although MPs could be interned, as was my friend Captain Ramsay, even the futile Morrison did not dare lay his hands on such a well-known member of the House of Lords.

After my release I did not visit the nuns, so as not to compromise them more, not knowing if they had been interrogated, but rang up the Reverend Mother, who was most reassuring to me. I have always found that the Irish have absolutely no contempt for prisoners of any kind and always sympathise with the under-dog; by comparison with the English they are much more humane and even courageous. I even remember in Ireland when I was a child a most respectable old nurse humming the words of the song 'A felon's cap is the proudest crown an Irish head can wear'.

The late Mgr Barton-Brown, my very dear and great friend, was the kind spirit who made all the arrangements for my journey to Ireland with the nuns, of whom he was the chaplain.

Chapter Nine

From Madrid to Suez

MADRID IS ONE of the cities of Europe which has always fascinated me most. The first time I arrived there was when my father took me at the age of about six – that is to say, in the early nineties, when Cuba was still a Spanish colony, which I only wish it had remained and which it might have done if it had not been for the unfortunate American interference which brought about the Spanish-American war which was so disastrous in its consequences.

Then a long period elapsed before I visited Spain again and in 1920 I went there at the request of three societies: Lord Parmoor's Fight the Famine Council which in turn sponsored the Save the Children Fund, and a branch of the Geneva Red Cross. My object in visiting Spain was to procure the support and sympathy of the Spaniards, and especially of the Royal Family, for the terrible plight of the German children in large cities like Leipzig. Today, with the Biafran victims, perhaps the horror of the German cities would not surprise anybody, but when I visited them, soon after the war, I was shocked and appalled.

It was that magnificent freedom fighter Emily Hobhouse who took me round the worst parts of Germany. I call Emily a freedom fighter not in the sense the term means in Africa today by those who assassinate harmless white farmers, but a real freedom fighter who fights for the under-dog in all countries and is an invincible

77

enemy of hypocrisy and cruelty. I wrote a long article in Germany about this lady for the *Frankfurter Zeitung* and later praised her on German radio. It may be remembered that the blockade of Germany was continued by the British for many months after the signing of the Armistice, but before the signing of the peace at Versailles, and this was responsible for the death and illness of thousands of German children. It was a most cruel and unnecessary action.

Spain in 1920 was very different from the Spain which I visited in my childhood. It was, as it is today, a very dignified country, the Roman Catholic Church having tremendous power and the Royal Family and the Army sharing some of this power, but by no means all. I had letters of introduction to everybody of importance in Spain. The British Ambassador I remember was Sir Arthur Harding, who was very helpful and kind to me and to whom I had a letter from his relative Henry Ponsonby, the brother of the then Lord Bessborough.

The Queen Mother of Spain was good enough to receive me almost on my arrival and at my audience, at her invitation, I showed her photographs taken in the hospitals and clinics of Germany. My audience lasted so long that the whole court was waiting outside in a row when the Queen commanded me to show the photographs to the waiting courtiers before they entered her Presence.

An amusing incident was that when one has an audience with the Queen Mother or the King or Queen of Spain, one is expected to carry one's top hat into the room with one. Unfortunately, being *en voyage*, I had no top hat but a felt one, which I attempted to hide under the seat on which I was sitting, but by the time I had bowed out of the room backwards, I found to my horror that I had left the hat behind. I have never seen it since.

The Royal Family were extremely welcoming and gave their support to various committees to help the German children. One court lady, rather an old harridan, the Duchess of Parcent, a German herself, was very bossy and tried to manage these committees. The Church was also helpful in its own rather tricky and subtle way. I had several audiences with the Archbishop of Toledo,

Cardinal Guisasola, and with the Bishop of Madrid-Alcala. At that time in Madrid there had arrived various Austrian priests, bent also on securing help for the suffering Austrian children. At the head of these men was Mgr Lastras, Chaplain to the Spanish Embassy in Vienna. It required great tact in order not to offend in any way this man, and at the same time to encourage support for those I represented. I must here say that the Queen Mother Maria Christina, herself an Austrian Archduchess and widow of Alphonso XII, was most kind and helpful and I had several audiences with her; I found she not only wished to do what she could for the Austrians, but was particularly impressed by the Save the Children Fund in England. I only wished that there could have been more royalty on the thrones of Europe like the Queen Mother of Spain.

I found the King jocular and merry and interested at the time in aviation. The Duke of Alba (who of course was also Duke of Berwick) was, I remember, announced at court as Duke of Berwick and Alba. The King turned to him and said in English, 'Why did you not call yourself the Duke of Alba and Berwick, you are a Spaniard?' The Duke flushed and said, 'Sir, if that is a command I will obey it, but if the choice is left to me I would still prefer to be known as the Duke of Berwick and Alba.' It may be remembered that the Duke inherited the Berwick title from his ancestor, who was the natural son of Arabella Churchill and King James II of England, and when the houses of Alba and Berwick intermarried, the title became joined. I remember also that when later on during the Second World War the Duke was Spanish Ambassador in London, the silver and china at his table all had the royal arms of England on them, crossed by the bar sinister. The present Duchess of Alba, who inherited the title from her father, was only a child at the time and I saw her only once at the Embassy. The Duke was very much angered by the murder of his brother, the Duke of Penaranda, by the reds who had taken him prisoner during the Spanish Civil War. Fortunately for the Duke, he was very deaf in one ear and this enabled him to sleep calmly at the Embassy during the many air raids on London that took place at that time. I cannot remember the details of all the very interesting conversations I had with him, but I do remember the long arguments about freemasonry. He told me he had dined the night before with Lord Lascelles and his wife, the Princess Royal, and that the former had told him that freemasonry in England had nothing whatever to do with freemasonry on the continent. I did my best to disabuse him of this fallacious idea and flatter myself that I succeeded chiefly by pointing out that the Pope would hardly put every freemason under the ban of excommunication if there really was a definite difference between British and continental freemasonry and that now the Ulster Lodges were in fraternal unison with atrocious lodges like the Grand Orient. Indeed, when Pétain came to power in France, one of his first actions was to have the premises of the Grand Orient in the Boulevard Haussman raided, and published in a Yellow Book what was found. I fortunately have a copy of this book which clearly proves the complicity of the Ulster Lodges with the Grand Orient in France.

But let us return to Madrid.

I was invited by General Queipo de Lana to visit him in Spain during the Spanish Civil War in Seville, but I declined the honour, although my sympathies were of course with General Franco. I have often been in Spain since and eventually in 1963 I decided to give up my small Chelsea house and settle permanently in Madrid. This I did, sharing a flat with an American friend for a year or two and later moving to a flat in the centre of the town, overlooking the back of the Spanish War Office. I wrote occasional articles and was twice interviewed on television. I was silly enough to follow a social life simply because I met so many interesting people – both Spaniards and foreigners. Madrid has always been a centre for exiled royalty. The Grand Duke Wladimir lives there and he is of course the only Russian who can claim the title of Tsar, being the son of the Grand Duke Cyril; his mother was the daughter of the Duke of Edinburgh and the grand-daughter of Queen Victoria. I had the privilege of meeting him on many occasions. Then again, thanks to a very kind friend, Prince Nicholas of Rumania, the only brother of the late King Carol, I met many other 'Royals'.

An English lady by birth, the Countess Buxhoevenden, entertained everyone lavishly at her famous apartment in the Avenida

Rosales. She had had an American husband before her present one and was extremely rich. She was not only sympathetic and charming to talk to, but knew everybody in the capital. Her great and most intimate friend at the time was Queen Geraldine of Albania, the widow of King Zog. This lady, an American by birth, was certainly one of the most beautiful and regal that I have ever met. The first time I had the privilege of meeting her was just after the publication of my book *Blood Royal* and the Countess had lent the Queen her copy. Very few friends were present and I was told that when the Queen came I was to sit next to her as she wished to talk to me about my book. As foreigners were present, the Countess reminded us not to start any topic of conversation but to let the Queen do so. While we were talking, a butler opened the door and an American friend of the Countess arrived unexpectedly. The Countess asked permission to present him to the Queen and then, although he was not expected that afternoon, he was told to sit down and served with drinks. After sitting there for some time, perhaps feeling that he did not receive enough attention, he suddenly said in a loud and squeaky voice, 'Say, Queen, did you hear the thunderstorm last night; it sure shook me'. The Queen replied quite calmly, 'We used to have very much worse ones in Albania'.

Whilst living in Madrid, I was twice interviewed on television by the distinguished Spanish broadcaster Sr Fernando Gayo. He paid me the compliment of coming to my flat with his television apparatus and technicians. I spoke of my love of Spain and of the various contrasts that Spain affords to most other European countries. Inevitably, the question was put to me: 'What do you think about Gibraltar?' I answered perfectly truthfully that I had of course studied the Treaty of Utrecht and in my humble opinion Gibraltar should become Spanish. After all it was God, or, if you prefer it, Nature, who defined the contours of the Iberian peninsula. Arrangements in the eighteenth century were purely temporary although it can be understood that in time of crises or war, in the old days, the rock provided a bastion of naval strength that it is understandable the British would insist on keeping. Today it has no military value whatever and is a constant thorn in the flesh of the Spanish Government on account of the limitless smuggling which goes on between Gibraltar and the Spanish mainland and now as Britain is so willing to hand back territories to various emergent African countries, there is no excuse for retention of this small stronghold. It must be remembered, however, that the British port had been obtained not by right of conquest, but by usurpation and emptied of its original Spanish population, all of which families live today in Spain, not in Gibraltar; it was lavishly repopulated with demographic groups, having no political entity, serving as employees of the base, always menacing and provocative in its behaviour towards Spain. It must also be pointed out that the UNO, never very friendly towards Spain, did decide, without a single contrary vote, that Gibraltar should be returned to the motherland. It is odd to think that the Wilsonian Government in England insists on other nations obeying the sanctions imposed by UNO against Rhodesia, but it chooses to ignore the UNO decision over Gibraltar.

The Spanish Government has always been ready to grant to the inhabitants of Gibraltar, not only suitable economic administrative rights, but a personal status in which their fundamental rights would be amply safeguarded, their British nationality respected, free exercise of their legitimate activities and retention of their posts of employment. However, the beginning of the negotiations in 1966 between the Spanish Minister of Foreign Affairs, Don Fernando Castiella, and Mr Michael Stewart, was broken off and resumed later without much headway ever being made. Matters came to a head again in June 1969 when the Spanish labour forec was withdrawn from the Rock. People are apt to forget that as a rule old Gibraltarian families no longer live on the Rock. Gibraltar is now populated by Indians, Arabs, Jews and even Yemeni. Of course I know that in the fullness of time Gibraltar will be returned to Spain, but it does seem to me tragic that all this time should be wasted and bad blood aroused between two countries who have every reason to be useful to each other.

Fortunately I have been all over Spain at various times and know most of the country. I stayed for a long time at the Colegio de los Nobles Irlandeses in Salamanca after the First World War. Most of the inmates were young Irishmen sent there to study and later to receive holy orders, but I was much impressed by the cordiality that existed between the Irish priests at this large college and the Spanish of the city. It is impossible to write about Spain without bearing in mind the tremendous power and beauty of the Roman Catholic Church there. Some of the ceremonies during Holy Week at the royal palace in the days of Alphonso XIII were unforgettable. I remember also walking along the Calle Alcala, not far from the royal palace, when a coach came down a side street, preceded by two little boys carrying red lights, which contained a priest bearing the Blessed Sacrament to a sick or dying person. The trams all stopped and most of the passengers knelt as the coach went by. At that moment from the royal palace appeared the King and Queen on their way to a bullfight, preceded by a royal escort of cavalry. When the King and Queen saw the two red lights indicating that the Blessed Sacrament was in the coach, they stopped their own carriage and sent someone to ask the priest to continue his journey in their carriage – an offer which was refused. A cloak was thrown on the ground and the King and Queen knelt for a few seconds to adore, and then rode on to the bull ring. The Queen I remember wearing a mantilla and large comb, suitable dress for a Spanish lady attending a bullfight.

Tired of life in London and before I went to live in Spain, I thought I would try Tangier and if I found I liked the town and climate, I would take a flat there. This I did in 1951. Tangier is inhabited, besides the Arab and Spanish population, by a number of well-to-do British and other European residents, most of them (I was told) having skeletons in their cupboards, which accounts for their presence on this hospitable North African shore. I stayed at first in the Rif Hotel, very solidly built – fortunately, as there was a mild earthquake a few days after I arrived, though I slept through it all, and even the sound of the disturbed skeletons in the cupboards of some residents did not wake me up.

There is a great deal to be said in favour of Tangier, just as there is a great deal to be said against it. Eventually, however, I took an apartment in the Rue Rembrandt. My presence in Tangier led to a variety of rumours as to what on earth had brought me to that wicked city. To the great disappointment of the café chatterers it was soon learned that I was only writing a weekly article for an American periodical, financed by the State Department and circulated all over North Africa, for the benefit of the hundreds of thousands of Americans working there building air bases and carrying out engineering undertakings.

Tangier is a city well known to almost every reader, thanks to innumerable Sunday-paper articles about the town. One of the journalists was introduced to me and after a week in Tangier he and his photographer went back to London and I was amused to read a little later the name of this reporter, followed by: '. . . Lifts the Lid off the Wickedest City in the World'. This exciting article was accompanied by two photographs – one of the Petit Socco and the other of a corner of the Kasbah, both of which could have been obtained from any post-card dealer for a few pence.

Actually, my own impression of Tangier during the two years I lived there was that there are few cities known to me which are more law-abiding than this town, and the International Zone of which at this time it was the centre.

There were, however, riots on one occasion, so unexpected in view of the good behaviour of the citizens that the police force were taken off their guard, especially as it was a Sunday. No serious damage was done, although some cars were smashed and burned, and one somewhat foolish young Swiss went into the crowd and received a bang on the head from which he afterwards succumbed.

When I heard the noise and saw a surging crowd of Arabs approaching, waving sticks and throwing stones, I was quite convinced that it was part of some film being made at that moment. So, unabashed, I later went out, to find the streets littered with the contents of looted shops: nylons, whisky bottles, shoes, leather goods. It then dawned on me that a real riot was taking place, and I was just close to the Spanish post office when I heard the rabble approaching once more, and a formation of police came charging down the street.

84

I fled down a side street, banged on the first door I could find, and was at once admitted with great cordiality. It was only when I got inside that I realised I had entered one of Tangier's best-known brothels, famous under its English name 'The Black Cat'. The Madame of the establishment said that it was most wise of me to take refuge, but hoped that I would not waste valuable time by sitting in the hall. Whether or not I was able to resist the blandishments of the attractive personnel can be surmised by those who know me best.

I made many new friends in Tangier. One of these, an eccentric but charming baronet, Sir Cyril Hampson, I particularly liked. I admired his erudition, his defiance of the shibboleths that ruled the English community, and above all his sense of humour. When somebody commented on the fact that I always got up in the morning before most people are awake (5.45 am), Cyril remarked, 'Of course he does. He can get so much more wickedness into the day like that.' Again, when we were in London, and on our way to dinner, it was suggested by another guest that we should go to a Chinese restaurant, but Cyril said, 'Oh no. Gerald always looks so cheated if he is taken to a Chinese restaurant when invited to dinner.'

When a very young man living in Paris, I used to see a lot of the then German Ambassador, Prince Radolin. The reason for this was that his wife was Jeanne Oppersdorff, the sister of a great friend of mine, Hans Oppersdorff, a fantastically rich Silesian magnate and the owner of Schloss Oberglogau, where I had often stayed. Prince Radolin always welcomed me and seemed to enjoy my visits, and I learned a lot of the strange ways of diplomacy from him. He was on the very worst of terms with the French Foreign Minister, Delcassé, but told me that whenever he received a letter from this gentleman, in spite of the contents, it always ended: '*Je suis de Vôtre Altesse Sérénisime le plus humble, le plus devoué et le plus obéissant des serviturs – Delcassé.*' This is the kind of diplomacy that I admire. Prince Radolin was in Germany a 'Durchlaucht', and one of the last mediatised princes.

The Prince's brother-in-law, Hans Oppersdorff, had married a Radziwill – the Princess Dorothy – and through her I met a great many other Radziwills who belonged to that rich aristocratic milieu which flourished up to the outbreak of the First World War. Through her I met the famous Princess Antoine Radziwill (her Christian names were Marie Dorothée) and her even more famous daughter-in-law the Princess Marie-Rose Radziwill. The elder lady was French born, but was so cosmopolitan, I remember, that it was quite impossible to realise what her nationality was. She was equally at home in Paris, Berlin, St Petersburg or Vienna. This Princess claimed to be the great-niece of Talleyrand. The German Emperor had a high regard for her, but with a touch of good-humoured contempt she made the observation that Talleyrand had made about Napoleon – 'What a pity that so great a man should be so ill bred.'

More interesting than her mother-in-law was Marie-Rose Radziwill – known to her intimates, and to me, as 'Bichette'. This Princess was a lady of great wit and knowledge, but unfortunately for her I remember she was enormously fat. Once when I was with her in Rome and she hailed a cabby, the driver with typical Roman humour said laughingly, 'I will have to come back and fetch the second half of you, as my horse is not used to such loads.'

The Peace of Brest-Litovsk caught Marie-Rose in her immense Polish estates near Warsaw, that part of Poland which had belonged to Russia; but she managed to get permission to journey to Rome. When the Second World War broke out, Bichette was back on her estates. Stalin's troops occupied her house, but she wrote cheerful letters, saying that they were kind and friendly, which is hard to believe, and carried her up and down stairs (no easy task!). The soldiers would stroll in and out of her room for an occasional chat, but were never conspicuously rude. I remember her telling me that one of the Russian soldiers, strolling into her bedroom un-announced one day, looked with interest at a crucifix above her bed and exclaimed, 'Is that a relative of yours being tortured?' The old lady died in 1941 and the last link of the old international set seemed to have been broken.

Before I leave my Radziwill friends, I must say a word about Prince Constantine Radziwill, who lived in Rome – or rather about his remarkable valet, a Frenchman called Albert Le Croziat. After the Prince's death this valet took over some baths in Paris called the 'Bains St Lazare', which catered for exiles of all kinds. Albert was, of course, an ardent Royalist and I remember having a meal with him at a bistro opposite his baths when the Emperor Carl of Austria was making his bid to regain his throne. An illustrated French newspaper had a large picture of the Emperor and his suite hearing Mass at a wayside station before reaching Vienna. Old Albert assured me that he was having a Mass said every day for the success of the Emperor's attempt.

The Suez Canal has recently celebrated, if that is the correct word, the 100th anniversary of its opening. For some reason the British Government always firmly objected to the whole scheme and at first would have no part in it. Lord Palmerston, Minister of Foreign Affairs and later Prime Minister, took violent exception to de Lesseps and all his ideas. The French Government, however, behaved warily but very firmly. The Emperor was advised not only by his Cabinet but also by the Empress Eugénie to support the idea and the Sublime Porte was also very careful. It must be remembered that Egypt at this time was a fief of Turkey and the ruler of Egypt was then called the Viceroy of Egypt. He was Mohammad Ali. His follower was Ismail, known as 'The Magnificent', for although almost entirely bankrupt, the wealth and luxury expended on the fêtes he gave were fantastic. He was created by the then Sultan of Turkey the first Khedive. Frank Harris once told me that he had been a close friend of the Khedive Ismail – whether true or not, I do not know.

Now to come to more recent times. On my way back from the Far East at the beginning of 1911, I stayed in Cairo for some weeks and was presented to the Khedive Abbas Hilmi II, a most sympathetic man of great charm and great cunning. He seemed to like me and put one of his magnificent cars at my disposal whilst I was in Cairo. This motor car had been a gift to him from Sir Ernest

Cassel and was certainly one of the most luxurious cars I have ever travelled about in. When the First World War broke out the Khedive found himself in Constantinople on a visit, which had been postponed, to the Sultan of Turkey, who was of course his liege lord. When Turkey decided to join the Germans the British of course attempted to find another nominal ruler for Egypt, who was called Sultan. Then came the King of Egypt, namely Fuad. I remarked that even if the British called him Pharaoh it would have no effect at all, as the legitimate ruler of Egypt was indeed the exiled Khedive.

When in Spain during the first part of this war, I met Prince Aziz Hassan of Egypt and a member of the Egyptian Royal Family, a close friend of the Khedive, but I never saw the Khedive again until the war was over and he was staying then in San Remo, where Aziz Hassan owned a sumptuous villa. The Khedive asked me to undertake various minor matters for him and after a certain time suggested that I should attempt to obtain from the Allies, or at any rate from the French Government, a permit for him to set foot on French soil. I found this very difficult, but Abbas Hilmi, who divided his time between San Remo and Switzerland where his great wealth was in one of the Swiss banks, assured me that money was no object and handed me a large sum to *'arroser le terrain'* in Paris. In the end, after a great many setbacks, I did succeed in getting him the required visa and we met again in Monte Carlo. In the meantime he had had a beautiful yacht constructed at Kiel called the *Nimet Allah*. I had the privilege of sailing with him in this yacht to various Mediterranean ports.

His one great object, however, was to regain a foothold in Egypt and this was quite obviously impossible at the time. It was hoped by various of his adherents that he would decide to settle in Paris, where I then lived. Relatives of his and the famous Princess Chewekar had even prepared an enormous blue leather book for callers to put their names down when he stayed in Paris. This Princess had been the wife of King Fuad of Egypt who, according to her followers, treated her so badly that her own brother, after quarrelling with him, attempted to shoot him dead, but the wound, a facial one, only had the effect of preventing the King from speaking clearly for the rest of his life. This Princess was not, however, the mother of Fuad's son, King Farouk.

All I have to add is my feelings of horror and shame when the Suez crisis occurred in 1956. On the occasion of Eden's dreadful blunder we were nearly precipitated into world war. Eden had apparently connived with Guy Mollet, the French Prime Minister, for a secret alliance which included Zionist elements in Palestine. Mollet was of course the prime instigator of this dangerous and disastrous piece of diplomacy because he wished to please the Grand Orient and other French masonic Lodges. The Jews only wanted to enlarge their territories in Palestine and disable Nasser and their enemies. Anyhow, had it not been for the prompt intervention of the United States, a continuation of hostilities, developing into a world war, would have undoubtedly ensued.

I will say no more about this dreary matter, because better pens than mine have gone into it so thoroughly, particularly the well-known Canadian author Terence Robertson, whose book *Crisis – The Inside Story of the Suez Conspiracy* has put the whole quasi-tragedy in its true perspective, and I am in agreement with every word Mr Robertson has written.

Chapter Ten

Italy and The Vatican

THE MOMENT THE First World War ended and I could take myself away from Paris (where I had gone as soon as a passport was issued to me) I returned to my most favourite place in the world – Sorrento. I had inherited a portion of the Villa Paradiso, where my mother's sister had resided, and immediately went there. I have described in other books the delights, amenities and disadvantages of life in Southern Italy shortly after the war.

I had been warned, for instance, that the postal service there was very unreliable, so one of my first visits was to the Sorrento post office, where I found the postman who would deliver my letters and explained to him the importance of receiving my mail punctually; I gave him a very handsome present and went back to the Villa. Next morning I, who am a very early riser as a rule, slept until quite late, being so tired after my journey from Naples the day before. The Signora Massa who was looking after me, a German lady by birth, waited for me to ring for my coffee and then told me the postman was waiting for me downstairs. I thought this must be a registered letter and was surprised one had come so quickly – but I asked her to bring him up to my bedroom. When he arrived, with much eye-winking and grinning, he emptied on to my bed the entire contents of his mail bag and suggested I choose any letters I wanted. He evidently thought I had some secret reason for wishing to interfere with the Sorrento mail in the district where the Villa was – otherwise he could not understand why I had made him such a handsome present. Amused, but yet appalled at what had happened, I quickly got rid of him and only hoped that the other recipients of mail that day had not been too distressed by the lateness of its arrival.

Speaking of the uncertainties of the Italian post reminds me of the story told me by the secretary of the Conte di Caserta in Cannes. At a time when the Italian censors used secretly to open all letters bearing the arms of the Neapolitan Royal House, the Count's secretary had occasion to send a remittance of two hundred lire to an old retainer in Naples. When the letter came to be opened by the censor there were no two hundred lire in it, as the secretary had forgotten to enclose them. The censor, however, supposing he himself had mislaid the amount and in order to avoid an incident, enclosed two hundred lire, expecting to find the original amount later on. The astonishment of the recipient may well be imagined when a day or two after receiving the first letter containing two hundred lire, he received a second one enclosing a like amount and the apologies of the Count's secretary for not having enclosed them in the first.

The Conte di Caserta was of course regarded by the Legitimists as the King of Naples and the Two Sicilies. He was a half-brother of Franceschiello, Francis II, the last reigning King, as he was called by his very loving subjects. Unfortunately, there was a feud between the Conte di Caserta and the widow of King Francis II, Maria-Sophia, who lived in Munich and blamed her brother-in-law for not urging the claims of the Neapolitan Royal House more actively and passionately than he did. The Queen lived until March 1925. I may presume to claim the title of being a close friend of hers.

When I went to Capri, which I often did, I found the fisher-folk who lived there referring to the Neapolitans as *'forestieri'*. This was of course in the days before Capri became the playground for the jet set which it is today. Norman Douglas, whom I had met before, was living there and my other friend was Count Adelsward-Fersen, the famous rich descendant of the man who tried to save Marie-Antoinette by acting as the coachman to the travelling *berline* the

Royal Family of France used when they tried to escape. Count Fersen was a unique character and became the hero or principal character of Roger Peyrefitte's famous book *L'Exilé à Capri*. He had had the misfortune when building his villa – called the Villa Lysis – to see a workman fall down a kind of precipice into the sea and killed. The superstitious inhabitants of Capri imagined he was under some curse. It was only after I got to know Count Fersen quite well that I found he was the first drug addict I had ever met. He took cocaine by sniffing it and seemed surprised when I emphatically refused to try to do the same. Through him, who was my host, I met a great number of people in Capri, which was just beginning to become a popular resort, but I did not care for those I met. The only person who interested me there was Maxim Gorky, who had just arrived from Russia. He spoke no Italian, French or English, but had a son who had some knowledge of these languages.

This Capri was a very different Capri from the one of today and I was always glad to get back to my quiet Villa at Sorrento. I really believe that, looking back on all my travels to so many near and distant countries, the drive from Sorrento to Ravello and Amalfi is one of the most beautiful in the world, and quite unforgettable.

In September of 1919 I received a letter from Monsignor Ceretti summoning me to Rome. This was in connection with my desire to obtain a private Audience with the Holy Father, in view of my work for the newly born Save the Children Fund. Before I left London I had been in touch with Lord Parmoor over his efforts to stop the blockade of Germany which was in full force at the end of the war, before the Peace Treaty was signed. In Germany it was called the '*Hungerblokade*' and was responsible for the death of innumerable children in Germany. This excellent effort of Lord Parmoor eventually gave way to the Save the Children Fund, and I was determined that the Catholic Church should intervene on behalf of these innocent victims of the war.

With the Pope's approval I felt that the movement to save the lives of the children of Europe, innocent victims of man's colossal folly in waging war, might assume enormous proportions, besides enhancing the power and prestige of the Church. Mgr Ceretti, who was later given a Cardinal's hat, was insistent that I should leave Paris for Italy, taking with me a letter signed by Lord Parmoor and addressed personally to the Pope. I was received by Benedict XV two days after my arrival in Rome. This was September 1919. I found him rather changed and aged by the terrible anxiety of the war. He, however, remembered me very well and listened with keen attention to what I said and the scheme which I propounded. He recognised at once, as I foresaw he would, the possible importance of my plan, which was to make use, with his consent, of the wonderful organisation of the Catholic Church for the efficient distribution of relief in the famine areas.

Although the Save the Children Fund was strictly undenominational and included upon its directing committee the Archbishop of Canterbury, Cardinal Bourne and the Chief Rabbi, it was admitted by all parties that only the Catholic Church could offer a wide, complete and practical international organisation which could adequately assist the rather few competent and experienced relief workers at the disposal of the Fund. The Holy Father asked me to prepare a detailed memorandum for his private perusal. He said as soon as Mgr Ceretti should return from Paris he would send for me again.

I remember a not unamusing little incident at this time. Before I left Sorrento, I had been to Naples to attend the ceremony of the renaming of the important thoroughfare leading from the port to the railway station. In future it was to be called the Via Presidente Wilson. The ceremony was elaborate; the street was blessed by the Cardinal Archbishop of Naples; the Sindaco (the Mayor) made a long speech and the imposing ceremonial continued – of which I have carried away only a hazy recollection of bright flags and quantities of incense; just before I left the street's name was duly unveiled. But in the short space of time between this ceremony and my departure from Naples to Rome, President Wilson had fallen very heavily from grace in the eyes of the Italian nation. As I drove down the street on my way to the station, I noticed, not entirely to my surprise, that the street's name tablet had been covered up and that a new sign now flapped in the wind bearing the words 'Via Fiume'. *Sic transit gloria presidentis.*

93

I broke my journey to Rome for a couple of nights at Monte Cassino, where I was for a few days the guest of the Benedictine Abbot. Most guide books will refer to the wonder of this monastery set upon a high mountain, but none can possibly convey to the traveller who has not been there himself an idea of this amazing edifice and the magnificent scenery which surrounds it. A visit to the library alone, to see the handwriting of St Thomas Aquinas and Duns Scotus, and to admire the superb colouring of the medieval missals, is unforgettable.

On reaching Rome my first visit was to Cardinal Gaspari, the Cardinal Secretary of State, who had always been very kind to me, and to Mgr Ceretti. I learned that the Holy Father was inclined to consider my memorandum favourably and desired me to elaborate certain details in accordance with his wishes. Again, the Pope received me in private Audience and this time I had an opportunity of showing him photographs of the emaciated and suffering children of Austria and Germany which lately had been sent to me from the clinics and hospitals of Vienna and Berlin. These pictures affected Benedict XV so deeply that he gave orders which enabled my plan of campaign to be put into immediate execution.

Throughout my negotiations with the Vatican, I had met with encouragement and support even beyond my hopes. From the very outset the Pope had fully appreciated the possible political importance of the Vatican's co-operation in the Save the Children Fund. Furthermore, Benedict XV had a great respect for Lord Parmoor, believing, like many other foreigners, that the debates in the House of Lords were of the utmost significance for English and European politics, and vastly more important than those held in the House of Commons.

The Pope once told me he had read most of Lord Parmoor's wartime speeches, as reported in *The Times*. He added that he was sorry these speeches, so illustrative of true Christian teaching, had been made by a member of the Church of England who was credited with extremely liberal opinions, and not by a Catholic peer, such as Lord Denbigh. The Pope had read Lord Denbigh's speeches also, and had found them disappointing.

After this audience with the Pope I gave an interview to the

Roman press upon the proposed scheme which, when published, aroused a great deal of comment. I left for Paris at the end of September to meet the various members of the Save the Children Fund, and to arrange for our concerted action.

At Paris it was decided that I should proceed at once to Germany, visit the slums of the larger cities and report on the conditions I found there. A small obstacle arose from the fact that my passport was specially marked 'Not Valid for Germany' – had this not been so I should most probably have gone straight to Germany as soon as I left England. I easily overcame the difficulty by going first to Berne, where a yellow *reiseausweis* was immediately issued to me, on receipt of instructions from Berlin, by the German Embassy and where the German Embassy provided me at the same time with a letter of recommendation to all customs and railway officials.

My emotion on setting foot in Germany for the first time in five years can be imagined. I will not harrow the reader by a description of the awful results of the blockade policy, but I declare that in the autumn of 1919, a year after the Armistice, the vast majority of the German people were on the verge of starvation, and that at least half a million innocent lives of babies and children were sacrificed to the wanton and hateful policy of continuing the blockade for half a year after the war had been concluded, and the Armistice signed.

It was always England's policy to sow as much dissension as possible between France and Germany; it has also been England's time-honoured policy to support the weaker of the two nations against the stronger, presumably to keep the balance even. Fifty years before, after Germany's victory, England slowly but surely veered towards France; the *Ententes Cordiales* of 1906 and 1907 marked the completion of this movement. After Germany's defeat in 1918 she supported her against France, so the pendulum swung and England sought only to avert a reconciliation. But if the Rhine, instead of being the barrier between two hostile neighbours, became the link between two utterly distinct yet in a sense complementary civilisations, where would England find herself? Not improbably shunned by both.

Before leaving Germany I had received a telegram from Cardinal Gaspari, confirming the Vatican's support for my projects. He further informed me that the Holy Father had ordered a collection in every Catholic church throughout the world on the last Sunday of December (appropriately enough, Holy Innocents Day) for the benefit of the Save the Children Fund. This telegram filled my heart with immense joy, and I gladly made my way to Geneva, where a general council of the various European relief committees was to take place.

The reason I showed such unwonted energy and enthusiasm in this matter is that I have always regarded children as a peculiarly sacred trust. What excuse can we offer if they are received by mothers unable to give them milk, by fathers crippled in war and unable to earn them bread, by want instead of nourishment, by hatred instead of love? In their hands and not in ours lies the future welfare of the world. The love of children should need no frontiers: whether they be French or German, English or Irish, Bulgarian or Rumanian, our duty towards them is the same, and our heavy load of responsibility is in no way diminished.

At Geneva it was decided to call a further general meeting in January, at which certain important matters were to be dealt with; it was decided also to establish a permanent office in Geneva to work under the aegis of the Geneva Red Cross.

I resolved on my way to Munich shortly after to accept for a few days the proffered hospitality of Prince Max of Baden, the last Imperial Chancellor, for whom I had always entertained a deep respect. I hoped to be able to include his name in the German Relief Committee.

The journey to Schloss Salem was both difficult and fatiguing. We were now in the depths of a peculiarly severe winter. I arrived at the castle feeling very ill and shaken. Prince Max received me most kindly, but showed very little interest in the schemes which I proposed to him. He complained frequently and bitterly that he had been betrayed by the Allies because, when he advised the abdication of the Emperor and the acceptance of the Armistice conditions, he had been given clearly to understand that Germany would be accorded easy peace terms and saved from further humiliation. Now he felt himself to be an object of suspicion among his own countrymen, who accused him of having given way too easily, and nicknamed him *'der rote Prinz'*. Although unwilling to take an active or prominent part in the relief work, he had already written a long letter to the Archbishop of Canterbury, under the remarkable impression that that dignitary could guide English public opinion to a better understanding of Germany's actual condition. The Prince gave me a signed copy of this letter (to which he had received no reply), but said that he considered the outlook to be hopeless and beyond repair. He wished only to withdraw from public life and to end his days in retirement.

His secretary, Kurt Hahn, an Oxford Rhodes scholar, later to become Headmaster of Gordonstoun, appeared on the morning after my arrival to say that the Prince wanted to know if I would care to play hockey. At first I thought this a joke, but then I remembered that, to the foreigner, every British subject must *ipso facto* be devoted to all forms of sport. I declined the invitation politely. Indeed, I felt anything but disposed for violent exercise. A latent internal trouble caused me excruciating pains; and the chilly castle, full of draughty passages and freezingly cold rooms, completed my discomfort. I was anxious to continue my journey, but instead was forced to go to the hospital in the small town of Überlingen on Lake Constance some thirty kilometres from Salem. There I was operated on completely successfully, but my recovery was not rapid. This was extremely irksome to me and the letters I received from Switzerland and Geneva increased my apprehension. But on Holy Innocents Day I did manage to drive to the church and contribute to the collection on behalf of the Save the Children Fund.

Naturally I received visits when convalescent from Schloss Salem. The old Grand Duchess of Baden, aunt to the German Emperor and mother of the then reigning Grand Duke, as well as of the Queen of Sweden, happened to be at Salem on a visit, and did me the honour of coming to see me.

Although very old, Louise of Prussia still retained complete control of her faculties, and was a forceful and determined old lady. Being, like all the Grand Ducal family, an ardent Lutheran, it grieved her to learn that I was a Catholic and shocked her even more to hear that the Blessed Sacrament had been carried to me in Schloss Salem on the day of my journey to Überlingen. Still, in spite of this shortcoming, I was afterwards assured by others that I had made a most satisfactory impression upon my august visitor.

When I eventually reached Geneva in the middle of January 1920, still very shaky after my illness, I was invited by the Save the Children Fund to proceed at once to Spain and to try to stimulate interest in our schemes there. I accepted this mission, knowing Spain and Spanish, but on the understanding that I should go first to Rome to obtain the approval of the Vatican. It was the end of January when I left Geneva for Rome. I had been warned not to undertake the journey in my delicate state of health as the Italian railway strike was in full progress and indeed, after reaching Domodossola, travelling became a nightmare. It lasted four days – the journey from Milan to Bologna taking fourteen hours alone, instead of the usual three. The stations were everywhere crowded with would-be travellers, waiting to hear if and when a train would leave for their destination. Bombs were not infrequently found on the lines, so that every train was full of soldiers in complete equipment as if going into battle. In fact, there seemed to be about three soldiers for every passenger – and Heaven knows there were passengers enough! Indeed, the trains were so long that it was a common joke to say one had only to walk down the train to arrive at one's destination.

We left Bologna one evening at six and reached Florence the next morning at four. In my compartment were no less than eighteen travellers and we all signed each other's notebooks as a souvenir of this memorable journey. Hardly surprisingly, I had to conduct my business in Rome from my bed.

It is difficult to remember incidents I have not put into either of my autobiographies, but, to go back a bit from the above events, when I was very young and a devout Catholic, my one ambition was to have an Audience with the Pope. At that time Pius X occupied the throne of St Peter. I obtained permission to present him with a clock that struck the angelus and after striking began the Latin prayer. This cost me a lot of money, but I was allowed to have a private Audience. The Pope, I heard afterwards, was very nervous because he spoke no language except Italian and that with a very strong Venetian accent. However, the only gift Heaven has given me and of which I am very proud, is my extraordinary facility to speak many languages – these include French, German, Italian and Spanish, which I profess to be able to speak absolutely perfectly and in three of these languages have constantly broadcast. The Pope was very relieved that I spoke Italian and, thanking me for the clock which he accepted most graciously, asked me how many lessons I had had in Italian to be able to speak it so correctly. I answered, most truthfully, that I had never had a single lesson but had easily learned Italian from several visits to that country. The Pope then looked surprised and said: 'My son, you are under the special protection of the Holy Ghost and you must make of Whitsuntide a special celebration.' As I knelt and kissed the ring of St Peter, I felt I was a very great hypocrite as I had learned Italian in anything but respectable company!

Shortly after the First World War, George Gavan-Duffy came from Rome to meet me at Genoa and we journeyed together to pay our respects to Gabriele d'Annunzio at his villa, called the Vittoriale, on the Lago di Garda. The poet had long shown great enthusiasm for Ireland's fight for independence and had a glowing admiration for Roger Casement. George Gavan-Duffy had of course been Casement's solicitor before he entered the service of the Free State, and I was known to be a close friend of Casement.

Anyhow, I was anxious to see the world-famous lover and poet and form my own opinion about this celebrated man.

On the whole I was very agreeably surprised. Certainly there was an element in his character which made him, consciously or unconsciously, a poseur. He even wore the garb of a Franciscan friar on most occasions.

We talked a lot about Casement and the state of Ireland at that time and he said, I remember, that 3rd August, the date of Casement's execution, should be for all Irishmen a day of *'ingino-chiato silenzio'*. As I spoke Italian and Gavan-Duffy only French, he asked me to translate the expression into suitable English and I interpreted it as a 'day of kneeling silence', which I thought a beautiful expression.

When we had finished talking about Ireland, we spoke of more mundane things and I was able to prove to him that I had read nearly all of what he had written and admired him more as a great poet than as a warrior. I remember asking him, as he was always considered to be a great aesthete, what was the most beautiful thing he had ever seen in this world. After some thought he remarked that there were three sights of equal beauty: they were the woods of Arcachon in the spring; the legs of Ida Rubinstein when she played San Sebastien; and lastly the eyes of his Arditi when they went into battle.

The King of Italy had recently created him Prince of Monte Nevoso and he showed us the official scroll which had reached him from Rome. I asked d'Annunzio whether he was proud to have received this accolade from the King and he said, rather arrogantly, that he merited much more from a not ungrateful Italy. He spoke perfect French and so was able to converse with Gavan-Duffy, who, I remember, told me he was bringing up his children to speak only French and Irish and no English at all.

One summer which I was spending in Italy I took a tiny cottage near the town of Lecco in Northern Italy, in order to write a book and to avoid the importunities of the British tax collector.

I noticed that the villagers treated me with great respect, much greater than I felt I was entitled to. I also noticed that I was constantly being asked in polite Italian fashion about the august health of King George. I always replied, thanking the enquirer, that as far as I knew he was very well and enjoyed good health. This reply seemed to satisfy them. One day the local parish priest, whom I knew, called to see me and, after beating about the bush, wondered whether I could possibly apply to the British Royal Family for funds for the upkeep of the local cemetery where several British tourists had been buried. I said at once that a letter from me about this matter would have no effect at all – why did he not write himself? The priest held up his hands – '*Ma che*, everybody knows that you are a close friend of the British Royal Family.'

Very surprised, I enquired how was that.

'Ah,' he said, 'the postman has told me about it.'

'About what?' I enquired.

'Well,' said the priest rather diffidently, 'the postman tells me you constantly receive letters from the King of England.'

I opened my eyes and said, 'I do nothing of the sort.'

'Yes,' he said, 'letters always come with "On His Majesty's Service" in big letters.'

I blushed at this unexpected link with the British Royal Family, remembering the British tax collector's tireless importunities!

Chapter Eleven

South Africa

IN 1959 IT was suggested to me that I should pay a trip to South Africa and write a book about my journey there and what happened to me. As I had never been to South Africa before, it was thought that an open mind would be able to write a book better than someone with political prejudices. The book was published by Sidgwick & Jackson under the title *Jacaranda*. I chose this word as I did not want to give the book a political title.

Great interest was attached to my visit to South Africa and to my surprise the first paragraph of the London Diary (which was the Editor's column) in the *New Statesman* of 19th December 1959 concerned my meeting with Field Marshal Montgomery in Johannesburg:

> The strangest pair of bedfellows political perversity ever made must surely be Field Marshal Lord Montgomery and Mr Gerald Hamilton. Whoever would have dreamed that these two would be found one day tucked up together, as it were, between the ideological sheets? The austerely hearty Monty and the ultra-sophisticated cosmopolitan 'Mr Norris', as Gerald Hamilton is affectionately nicknamed on account of the fancied – and purely imaginary – resemblance between himself and his friend Isherwood's famous character. It is the sort of fantastic juxtaposition you might expect to find in a *New Statesman* competition or a game of Consequences. Yet here they are together in real life espousing the cause of the

South African government and apartheid. Both have been visiting the Union. Gerald Hamilton is still there. Like the swallows, he prefers to winter in a warm climate whenever possible. He is expressing cautious sympathy for the South African government, which, he suggests, has been much misunderstood. His friends, who have always been careful to separate Gerald Hamilton's political vagaries from the rich, timeless compost of his personality, which has been compared to a paté unusually well stuffed with truffles, will be amusing themselves reconstructing snatches of dialogue between the two venerable ideologues.

'Everything is all tickettyboo, Hamilton, don't fuss! These Dutch chaps have got the Bantu properly buttoned up.'

'I'm so glad to hear you say that, Field Marshal. You relieve my feelings immensely.'

I spent nine months in South Africa and visited every town of importance. At that time I was neither right wing nor left wing, but I gradually became enthusiastic over the conditions I found and was particularly surprised to find the Bantus not only not oppressed at all, but all seeming very cheerful. The shanty towns had been destroyed and new buildings in the suburbs had just been erected, each family having a small cottage with a tiny garden. This was very different from what I had been led to believe by my left-wing friends in London.

The famous Father Huddleston was of course attacking the government on every occasion he could and, therefore, I felt it my duty, when speaking on radio, to emphasise the good points of the South African administration. The whole question of *apartheid* is more complicated than it at first appears, but after my visit to South Africa I am quite certain that it is in that country's interest that the present laws should continue. There is no question of the black South African being oppressed, but in my view they are not yet capable of taking part in the government.

I made the acquaintance of Chief Luthuli who was under house arrest at the time and the government suggested it was not worth my while to visit him. However, when I was in Durban I managed to get an Indian to pick me up at my hotel, in the middle of the night, and to take me and a photographer to the village of Stanger in Zululand. Word had been sent to Luthuli that I was coming and he was to meet us at the end of a road. Needless to say, there was one of those tropical downpours which are common in Natal in the summer and it was the month of December. The Indian arrived with the car, late, and poor Chief Luthuli was drenched by the time we had covered the sixty miles or so to Zululand.

I felt the greatest admiration for this valiant man who was later awarded the Nobel prize on account of his opposition to the South African Government, coupled with his insistence that this opposition should be a peaceful one. At times he spoke under stress of strong emotion, and then particularly I felt a kind of affection for him. He was so obviously sincere and had given up everything that made life agreeable in order to further his opinions and to fight for what he considered the rights of the Natives of South Africa. I do not agree with any of his reasons for opposing the government so forcibly, but must admit that he was an exceptionally gifted Zulu chief. I have written in my book all I wanted to say on this matter and will not repeat myself.

I found the fact that I had been a close friend of Emily Hobhouse to carry much weight during my stay in the Union. She had impressed me so very much when I had met her after the First World War when we were both engaged on relief work in Germany, that I considered it a privilege to have remained her friend until her death. She is remembered and loved in South Africa for her kindness and bravery during the Boer War when she agitated against the conditions in the concentration camps in which South African women and children were confined. With the help of Lloyd George she had drawn attention to the appalling conditions, but on her return to South Africa found Lord Kitchener in command. He had a strong dislike of women, but Emily Hobhouse could claim to take the lead and he did not care even for her name to be mentioned and referred to her as 'that bloody woman'. His aides amongst themselves called her 'TBW'!

I was in South Africa at the time of the Sharpeville incident when many Africans were fired upon and killed. I could hardly believe my eyes when I saw the versions that appeared in the British press accusing the South African Government of ordering police to fire on an unarmed South African crowd merely because they were destroying their passes – identity cards that every Bantu must carry. Actually, what took place was that an enormous crowd of Africans, I believe something like sixteen thousand, advanced upon a small police station at Sharpeville, threatening to kill all the police who were there. The police, in view of the numbers and because the crowd would not disperse, had orders to fire to defend their lives. One wonders who it is who deliberately distorts the facts of any incident of shooting to their own political colour.

It is impossible to view a tragedy like that in a detached way and I do not know what a hundred and fifty policemen are supposed to do when they believe they are about to be attacked by sixteen thousand or more; I daresay the constables with the guns in their hands that day didn't know either. But I think, to make a fair judgment, it is necessary to consider the factors which surrounded this incident. In recent times British colonial policy and the treatment accorded African affairs, particularly by the British press, have brought the white man in Africa into disrepute and have led the black man to suppose there is nothing to which he cannot lay claim. Little men with loud mouths have been raised overnight by popular press and television to international fame, and surely every tin-pot agitator in Africa must cherish a real hope that his name may burst the day after tomorrow across Fleet Street's front pages. It must be admitted that much was emanating from Britain to encourage ambitious Africans to resist law and order.

It was since my return that the Rhodesia question occurred and my book *Jacaranda* purposely did not refer to Rhodesia on the publisher's instructions.

I was left entirely independent in South Africa, to go where I wanted to go, except of course to visit politicians who were under house arrest, and being a member of the Howard League for Penal Reform I visited the leading prisons in South Africa. Of course prisoners are segregated and I would like to quote from my book this account of my visit to Leeukop prison for non-whites:

> The cleanliness and the sanitary arrangements and the general
> air of cheerfulness, instead of despair, on the faces of the Native

prisoners at Leeukop compared more than favourably with the overcrowded insanitary and old-fashioned institutions in which prisoners are confined in England today.

As I and the two friends who accompanied me drove in through the gates of Leeukop we seemed to be entering the drive leading to some important country seat. Large gardens with flower beds making a riot of colour lay on each side of the drive, and when we at last reached the central buildings we were greeted not by a prison governor, as would have been the case in England, but by a very charming, merry but efficient police captain who was in charge.

Prisoners in the Union were graded A, B, C, and D. The A and B category in the Transvaal were sent to Leeukop, whereas the more dangerous C and D were sent to other prisons. The immense tract of country surrounding Leeukop is used for farming of all kinds and in the workshops all the equipment for the farm was made – as well as fittings for Government offices. The living conditions of the prisoners I described:

> There were cold-water showers and up-to-date flush toilets in every dormitory, and spacious sisal mats on the floor on which the prisoners sleep. (The average Bantu regards a bed with both suspicion and dislike and has all his life slept on mats probably less comfortable than the ones provided at Leeukop.)
>
> Every Saturday each prisoner is provided with a complete change of all clothing, and a bath is compulsory. More frequent baths can be had if necessary and when asked for. Blue coats are provided for habitual criminals, and white coats for indeterminate sentences. Three ample meals are provided each day, cooked in modern steam cookers, and during the first six months of the imprisonment most prisoners put on an average of 20 lb in weight. . . .
>
> On completion of sentence, jobs are found for prisoners before they leave the settlement, through the good offices of the South African Prison Board.

In Transvaal they also have an institution unique in the Commonwealth at that time and this was a Boys' Town set in two thousand acres of farmland opened in 1958 for boys to be sent to find a new purpose in life – and they come from many different backgrounds: orphans, results of broken homes, or incipient juvenile delinquents. The boys belong to all denominations and are trained for responsible positions when they leave. They elect their own officers – including a mayor – and generally run their own affairs. I was particularly impressed with the good manners of all the boys I spoke to.

To round off this tour of 'institutions', I must just mention Baragwanath Hospital, outside Johannesburg, which is exclusively for Natives and supported by the Government. In all truth and simplicity I can say that I could never have imagined any more complete and beautiful hospital to have existed anywhere. It is very vast, and fitted with every possible sort of modern equipment. A feature which especially impressed me was the importance attached to occupational therapy for cripples and paralysed people who seemed most cheerful and happy.

Personalities: I think I liked Mr Paul Sauer (then the most senior Minister next to Dr Verwoerd) better than any other Ministers I met, and could not decide which interested him most – politics or wine – and it was in this last connection that I particularly spoke to Mr Sauer. He was very keen to introduce a cheap, young, honest-to-God wine for the poor man to drink as a substitute for beer. Dr Verwoerd I did not meet personally but I wrote at the time of my visit to South Africa:

> He is supremely self-assured . . . this is at the same time his strength and his weakness. He is very pleased to listen quietly and thoughtfully to the views of others – but there is not a shred of evidence I know of that he is prepared to change his on anything fundamental. One can only hope that they are right and good for South Africa because one thing is certain – as long as he is in power they will be implemented.

Another personality I met in Johannesburg was Mr Tom Hopkinson, who had been for a long time editor of *Picture Post* in London. He was then editor of the African illustrated monthly *Drum* and the various editions for different African countries totalled a quarter of a million copies sold each month. Mr Hopkinson's view on *apartheid*, which he thought wrong, was that it would gradually disintegrate. As he saw it, the real tragedy is that the Natives are wanted as workers but not as human beings.

Of the major towns I visited, my impressions of each, in a nutshell, were: Cape Town I found the most agreeable and the surroundings at times dazzlingly beautiful. Durban I considered the least attractive, certainly the least sympathetic of South African cities – the average Durban citizen of British stock is snobbish to a degree. The atmosphere of Pretoria struck me as being different from that of any other city in the Union – it seemed to have a peacefulness, a serenity and a dignity that the larger, bustling cities of the Union lacked so completely. The amazing thing about Johannesburg is the fact that about seventy years ago it did not exist; it is built like an American city with the streets constructed with right-angled intersections. I felt it was one of the most modern and vital cities I have ever visited and I left with feelings of regret.

Chapter Twelve

Royal Families

IN A book of mine published in 1964, called *Blood Royal*, I hardly referred to the British Royal Family – partly out of my deep respect for them and their extremely difficult and so often vulgarly criticised activities. A little while ago there appeared in the *New Statesman* a profile of the Queen which at first rather shocked me, but later brought a gleam of admiration into my eyes as I read on further.

Whether it be true or not, as the writer of this profile alleges, that our present Queen has three interests in life: horses, dogs and Dukes – and in that order – the fact remains that Queen Elizabeth II is the Queen of England and entitled to the respect, love and affection of her subjects. As an Irishman, however, I may venture perhaps to be more critical than I would be were I a devoted British subject of Her Majesty.

One thing is certain and that is that no-one else but the present Royal Family has any right to the throne of Great Britain. It is true there are many sentimental Stuart sympathisers who doubt this and I myself for a certain time as a very young man regarded the Princess Ludwig of Bavaria as legitimate Queen of England owing to her direct descendance from Charles I. I even went to Munich on a two-fold royal visit – one was to pay my respects to this gracious lady – but was warned beforehand by Herr von Lassberg, her Oberhofmeister, never during my audience to refer to those in England who might regard her as their Queen. My other royal visit at the time was to Maria-Sophia, the last Queen of Naples, who did not die until 1925 and who figures largely in my book *Blood Royal*.

I quite truly had a most unstinted admiration for King Edward VII, partly because he was a man of the world, and largely because he genuinely did manage to keep peace in Europe, and finally for having brought about the *Entente Cordiale* with England's arch-enemy, the French Republic.

His son, however, King George V, failed to awaken these sentiments in my pro-Royalist heart. A man of undoubtedly below the average intelligence, of stern principles and loyal to friends up to a certain point, King George was a man of limited vision. Anybody who has read Sir Harold Nicolson's *Life of King George V*[1] will have noted the force of what I am saying. In a letter to his wife dated 17th August 1949, when he was writing the Life of that King, Sir Harold wrote:

> I fear that I am getting a down on George V just now. He is all right as a gay young midshipman. He may be all right as a wise old king. But the intervening period when he was Duke of York, just shooting at Sandringham, is hard to manage or swallow. For seventeen years he did nothing at all but kill animals and stick in stamps.

I do not think the King ever wrote many letters, but the few that exist in that strange school-boy handwriting really have no importance. But my real quarrel with the King begins with the way he abandoned the Imperial Russian Family at the time of the disastrous Russian Revolution. Kerensky was finally persuaded to inform the British Ambassador, Sir George Buchanan, that he would allow the Imperial Family to go to a Baltic port to be picked up there by a British man-of-war. King George professed to be delighted at this and then Lloyd George intervened. With regard to Lloyd George I adopt a fairly neutral attitude. There is no doubt that he was involved in the sale of titles and honours; on the other hand, at the beginning of the Second World War he did his

[1] *Life of King George V*, Harold Nicolson.

level best to instil some sense into the crazy brains of the British Cabinet and I was enabled (thanks to his assistant Mr Silvester) to have one interview with Mr Lloyd George in my wild anxiety to have the war stopped; I was gratified by this statesman's agreement with much of what I said. However, at the time of the Russian Revolution Lloyd George undoubtedly succeeded, perhaps no difficult task with such an irresolute man as was the King, in dissuading him from sending help to Russia to save the Imperial Family from the appalling death that awaited them so soon after. I attribute the murder of the Imperial Russian Family to a large extent to the dilatoriness and lack of decision of the King. For this reason I have no high regard for him or his interventions.

Later, it is true, when the Emperor and Empress of Austria found themselves in a predicament similar to that of the Russian Imperial Family, when Prince Sixtus of Parma, the Empress Zita's brother, obtained an audience with the King and Queen Mary and asked them to help the endangered Austrian Imperial Family who were suffering every hardship at the end of the war, thanks to Queen Mary's urgent plea to the King, the King decided he would do what he could. He entrusted a delicate mission to Lieut-Colonel Strutt, who, partly through bluff and partly through his own great skill and capability, managed to save even some of the jewels of the Imperial Family, stuffing the Empress's pearls into a pocket and other jewels into another. He accompanied them to safety in Switzerland. After the death of the Emperor Karl in Madeira I was privileged to have an interview of the Empress Zita, an honour I shall never forget.

The full story of King George's eldest son is so well known, so much has been written by better pens than mine, that I will limit myself to my own viewpoint. Like all Hanoverian monarchs, whose feuds with their eldest sons belong to history, King George V was never on good terms with his eldest son. When it was found that the Prince of Wales as King was never willing to sign on the dotted line as had been his predecessors, a camarilla containing members of the British Establishment was soon formed and headed by Baldwin and Archbishop Lang, that Caiaphas of Canterbury, and King Edward VIII was hounded into exile. It is obvious that the

Duke of Windsor, even when King, would never wish to make the charming Mrs Simpson his mistress, but I do not see why he never consented to making a morganatic marriage, even if this would have been at first objected to by a good many of his countrymen. The parallel occurs to me of the difficulties the Archduke Franz Ferdinand of Austria, heir to the thrones of Austria and Hungary, had when he wished to make a morganatic marriage. Naturally the old Emperor objected very strongly, as did the court camarilla. Nevertheless, the Archduke persevered and finally married the lady of his choice, which was a most happy marriage, and the Emperor not only forgave him but took him into his affections once again. If it had not been for the bullets at Sarajevo, the Archduke would no doubt have made an excellent monarch.

The treasonable acts in connection with the abdication of King Edward VIII were only clear when, after the Second World War broke out, it was obvious to those in the know that had the real King occupied the throne, this war might never have broken out at all. The King was a man of the world and able to judge politically more easily than his brother, King George VI. The whole attitude of the Royal Family seems to me to have been beyond contempt; even Queen Mary, for whom I have always had a sneaking regard, referred always to the Duke of Windsor in conversation as 'my poor son', as if he had some terrible disability. The studied disapproval of all members of the Royal Family has even now hardly shown signs of diminishing.

A word must be said now about the Duchess; about the dignity she has always shown; about her loving tenderness to her husband, and her great tact and loyalty in the most difficult situation the wife of any King or ex-King in the history of England has had to contend with. The constant snubs, the refusal of the court to receive the ex-King's wife, whose behaviour had always been admirable, leave a nasty mark on the escutcheon of the British Royal House. It may be argued that I personally have a special respect for the Duke of Windsor because on the publication of my book *Blood Royal* he wrote me a very charming letter of congratulations. As a Monarchist, I dislike any interference with a dynasty whose rule is that the title of King goes from father to son and I consider the loss to England by driving the Duke of Windsor into a despised exile and forcing him to marry the lady of his choice in a hole-and-corner manner in France, is one of the most distressing and ugly pictures the history of England has to offer.

A friend of mine who, contrary to my advice, joined the Irish Guards during the war became a national hero. His name was Pat Kenneally and as a sergeant at the Battle of El Alamein performed the heroic feat, it was claimed, of killing several Germans and was awarded the VC. When he came to London to receive this honour, he was good enough to invite me and his mother to attend the ceremony of Investiture at Buckingham Palace. Curious as ever to see the workings of such ceremonies, I accepted the offer and accompanied his mother and him from Chelsea Barracks to Buckingham Palace. As we were rather late and quite at the end of the queue of those to be decorated and their friends, to my surprise the Lord Chamberlain, after telling us what to do should there be an air raid, asked that those who accompanied Sergeant Kenneally should stand up; I said to his mother, 'This is because they intend to turn me out', to which she said, 'In that case I shall go too'. However, this was not the case, but that the King wanted us to sit on seats in the very front row, as there had been tremendous propaganda praising Sergeant Kenneally. I was very careful to tell Kenneally what I thought about the matter – today this would be called brain-washing no doubt. I was not in agreement with any fellow countryman of mine enlisting in the British Army to fight England's battles and as for killing all the Germans he did kill, they had mothers and fathers just as he had. Being a VC he took precedence over his own officers and others at the Investiture and when the King said to him 'Your parents and friends must be very proud of you', he dared to say that there was one with him who thought he was no better than a murderer. The King shook his hand and said good-bye.

I have tried to avoid mention of names of such royal people as I had the honour of knowing, because I have said more than enough about all these in my previous book *Blood Royal*. However, one or two small incidents are worth remembering.

One is that when King Carol of Rumania lived in Paris in exile with Madame Lupescu, whom it may be remembered he married much later in Brazil, French authorities and friends were careful to give this lady the status of a King's mistress, but protocol demanded that in public this lady should curtsy to the King and address him, if in French, as 'Sire'. The good lady, however, outraged public opinion in Paris by never curtsying and actually 'tutoying' him. This shocked everybody and did the King a tremendous amount of harm.

Actually it was at Deauville in the summer of 1921 that I met his father, King Ferdinand, known as 'Nando', when I was sitting on the terrace of the 'Potinière' with Herr von Hoesch, later German Ambassador in London, where he died, who asked permission to present me to the King, who was accompanied by a Rumanian gentleman. I though what a contrast there was between the King – he seemed very insignificant – and his ebullient wife Queen Marie, whom I had only then met once, in Bucharest, and who, I felt, rather disapproved of me. She was in the full bloom of her beauty at that time and had all the treatment which a film star would have today. She was not only a beautiful woman, but a wonderful rider and proud of her two sons, although of course Carol caused her tremendous sorrow. Prince Nicholas, Carol's only brother, as I mentioned in a previous chapter, was a close friend of mine but never on very good terms with his brother and is today on the worst possible terms with Madame Lupescu.

I can claim to have been a fairly close friend of King Constantine of Greece, the grandfather of the present King, and when he was in exile just after the First World War I was his guest at the Hotel National in Lucerne. His sister, the Grand Duchess George of Russia whose husband had been murdered by the Bolsheviks at the time of the Revolution, lived in London and I saw a good deal of her. She had been welcomed by Queen Alexandra and occupied a lovely house near Regent's Park. She was devoted to her brother and had spoken of me to him in letters and I was then asked to join him and his court in Lucerne, which I did. His private secretary, a Mr Stein, lived in another hotel almost opposite the National and any usefulness I had was to suggest ways and means of getting suitable paragraphs in the English and French papers. I flatter myself I succeeded in doing this with admirable speed and good results. I did not see the King every day of my stay, but was often commanded to his table and grew particularly fond of the Queen, who was a sister of the German Emperor. Also present with the Royal Family were the Diadoque, afterwards King George II, and Prince Paul who reigned after his brother who left no issue, and who was the father of the present King. Finally, the King returned to Athens sometime after I had left Lucerne, sailing from Trieste, and received a most tremendous welcome on his return. Everything went well for a time, but the Athenian mob is fickle and some years later poor King Constantine had to go once more into exile and finally died in Palermo.

All this is a prelude to my dislike of that atrocious statesman Venizelos, who did nothing but thwart all my humble efforts to help King Constantine and who might be said to be responsible for driving the Royal Family into exile. Venizelos was a most unscrupulous intriguer but very unfortunately succeeded in acquiring excessive influence over Lloyd George, chiefly by flattery but also by extreme cunning. Everybody who knew the circumstances agreed with me on this point. Lord Vansittart, for instance, quoted by David Walder in his book *The Chanak Affair*, said:

> The Cretan was the worst influence in Lloyd George's life and in the end its undoing. He was a courteous fox, an affable barmecide of reason, the best foul-weather friend we ever had . . . I admired and distrusted him immensely.

Certainly, had it not been for Venizelos and his influence on British politicians, King Constantine might never have had to go into exile. His great fault in the eyes of the Allies and in Venizelos's followers' was that he wished to keep his kingdom absolutely neutral during the First World War and resisted the blandishments of the Allies to allow his army to march under their flag.

Chapter Thirteen

Food and Drink

I HAVE BEEN rather looking forward to writing this chapter since starting my book, as I consider food and drink to be as important as any other subject-matter in the world of today. My theory is, and always has been, that people eat far too much – also they drink more than is necessary, even abstemious people. I attribute the good health I enjoy at the age of over eighty partly to the fact that as a general rule I find one substantial meal a day is ample. This I usually like at mid-day, but if I am dining out I have a light snack at mid-day and look forward to my evening meal.

A pet theory of mine is that a good cook is just as worthy of the highest honours as a great poet, a great painter or a great composer. The art of cookery is certainly on the same level as these other arts and history is full of instances of the loyalty and devotion of good cooks to their masters. It seems very odd to me that such a wonderful gift should pass comparatively unappreciated in the world of today, when honours are lavished on artists in other spheres.

Ever since I was a boy I have been interested in food and I remember my parents' surprise when they received my first report from my prep school, Lambrook, near Bracknell, and the headmaster's comments were limited to the words: 'Shows unusual intelligence for his age, but unfortunately is such a greedy boy.' Well, the greedy boy grew up and was one of the first to join the

Wine and Food Society at its very beginning, and the greedy boy gained a reputation for his discerning palate as well as for his knowledge of wines.

In order fully to appreciate wines I was obliged, of course, to give up smoking, as I cannot possibly believe a smoker can judge good wines. True, André Simon, who objects to cigarette smoking and of course pipe smoking, does allow himself a cigar after a good meal – and who am I to criticise the Master? I do not even smoke cigars myself, but I must say in their favour after one or two have been smoked in the room, I appreciate the capitalist odour of a Corona Corona!!

I have expressed my horror of people who have so little regard for good wines that they are barbaric enough to smoke while wines are on the table. My father, who was a great cigar smoker, always retired to a different room before smokes were lit and allowed no-one to smoke in the dining-room for fear the wines – especially the port – might be affected. I myself used to smoke cigarettes, but gave them up forty or fifty years ago and have never resumed this pernicious habit. Indeed, when I had a bigger house in London a large notice hung in the sitting-room – VISITORS ARE REQUESTED NOT TO SMOKE IN THIS ROOM. It was only when once I had to go to the bathroom and had come back and found my guests all sniggering because one of them had managed to scratch out the 'SM' of smoke and replace it with a 'P', that the notice was taken down.

So great, however, was my keenness to persuade wine drinkers that they should give up smoking if they wished to appreciate their wines that I joined the National Society of Non-Smokers and one year was elected Chairman. At the Annual Meeting at Caxton Hall that year I found myself confronted by a large number of clerical gentlemen, who, when they rose to speak, one and all bracketed non-smoking with teetotalism. When I could bear this no longer, I tapped loudly with my gavel and rose to say that if I had given up smoking it was only so that I could appreciate wines more; that this was a Meeting of the Society of Non-Smokers and had nothing at all to do with teetotalism, and anyhow the reverend gentleman who had just spoken must evidently have forgotten the scriptures, because quite apart from St Paul's recommendation – 'Above all, drink no longer water but use a little wine for thy stomach's sake and thine oft infirmities' – Our Blessed Lord, at the marriage feast in Cana of Galilee, did not change the water into tea or some repellent soft drink, but into good healthy red wine. No one seemed to wish to rise to argue with me about this, and so the meeting passed off quietly. But it is a fact that in some English brains non-smoking and non-drinking seem to be united.

In my opinion, smokers are the most selfish people on the face of this earth; they seem to have no understanding, still less any regard, for the comfort and feelings of those with them; they light cigarettes almost under the noses of other people without as much as an 'Excuse me!' or 'Do you mind my smoking?' Meals and tempers are equally spoilt by this outrageous conduct. Once at a luncheon party sitting next a young peeress who lit a cigarette when the lunch began, I somewhat ostentatiously waved my handkerchief in the air; she turned to me and said, 'Oh, do you mind my smoking?' I replied, 'Dear lady, if you would only smoke I would mind much less, but since you have lit it you have held it in your hand and not put it near your mouth and all the smoke has gone into my eyes and food.' On another occasion when some barbarian had lit a cigarette at table, I politely enquired, 'Do you mind my eating while you smoke?'

I consider wines more important really than food, though I suppose I ought to admit they are both of equal importance; but when I had money and a large household, I used first of all to decide what wines I would get from the cellar for a dinner party according to the eventual guest or guests; after the wine had been decided, I would then consider the menu to match the wines. I know that most people prefer to think of the menu first and the wines after, but I prefer my own way of doing things. Actually, when I had a charming house in Kinnerton Street at the beginning of the last war and a wonderful cellar of my own, thieves broke in and stole my valuable wines, and I was told by the police it was the first robbery on record when only wines were stolen. Nothing was touched in the house – just the contents of my precious cellar. A newspaper report on 10th May 1941 said :

CID officers were today looking for a gang of thieves who are connoisseurs of wine.

The thieves broke into a house in Kinnerton Street, Knightsbridge, last night and removed the valuable contents of the wine cellar.

Among the wines stolen were vintage Burgundies, Clarets and Champagnes, including some bottles of '06 Château Mouton Rothschild and 1916 Burgundy. The thieves also took bottles of fine old brandy and some old Green and Yellow Chartreuse valued at 8 guineas a bottle.

With the present scarcity of French wines they will have little difficulty in selling this haul.

The owner of the wines, Mr Gerald Hamilton, was in the country when the thieves raided his cellar.

So much has been written lately by worthier pens than mine about wine and the wine trade that it seems a little unnecessary for me to write too much on this entrancing subject. The trouble in London today seems to be that, judging from what happens to my friends, too many people seek good wines at prices they cannot afford and then are obliged to consume inferior wines at prices they can afford.

My reputation had gained considerably during the last war and I was invited by the Editor of a well-known weekly paper *Everybody's* to write a weekly article for three months on food and drink. Rationing was, of course, in force but in spite of this, I never enjoyed myself more than when I was writing these articles, because I was able to launch attacks on things to which I objected, and commend pet ideas of mine. As I cannot cook, my friends were amazed to hear I had this contract and lady friends rang each other up – 'My dear! Have you heard the latest? Gerald is writing about cookery – as you know, he can't cook an egg by himself and once asked me what to do with some sausages.' It is of course a fact that I know little about cooking, because it is the finished article which interests me.

With regard to wines, only long study and a perfect palate can decide which wines are good and which are not. I was privileged once to be the guest of Sir Denison Ross just before he left for Istanbul, where he died. We had dinner at the Ritz – a party of eight, whom he had chosen as the most knowing claret lovers in London. He brought his own wines to a private room at the hotel and the food had been selected to match these wines. Actually, he had a few bottles of pre-phylloxera Lafite – both 1864 and 1870. He warned his guests that he could not be sure in what state the wines would be found – they might have deteriorated into a sweet syrup – or they might be quite wonderful. The bottles were duly opened and allowed to take the air for a bit; their temperature was perfect; then he said, 'Now, let us taste this wine.' I can never remember tasting anything more wonderful. After commenting on our first glass, which was so delicious, and the glasses had been changed, we embarked on the second glass of the same wine. A look of horror spread over our faces – the wine had died. No doubt the oxygen in the air was strong enough to destroy its taste after being bottled for so long. No-one seemed to know what to say, so I tried to save the situation by remarking that anyhow it was an honour to have assisted at its obsequies.

When I was in South Africa in 1959 and 1960 I was lavishly entertained by the KWV, which is the greatest and most powerful wine co-operative in the country. I was shown the fabulous wine-cellars at Paarl where one can, if one wants to, walk for miles between the enormous vats, the biggest of which hold as much as 45,000 gallons and were built in Portugal in the eighteenth century. The more usual sized vats are the Stukvats which hold 2,600 gallons each and are made of oak. Sherries and brandies are the two specialities there and I thought them both really excellent. The brandies are usually three, five or ten years old, and though this may sound very young to those accustomed to older French brandies, it must be remembered that maturation takes place much quicker in the climate of South Africa. I certainly found the ten-year-old brandy which I had at Paarl very good indeed.

At the Nederburg wine farm I found some of the finest hock type wine I have drunk outside Germany. At another estate I was surprised to find a *vin rosé* offered me as an aperitif before lunch so delicious; although it looked like *vin rosé*, it did not remind me of the product which usually goes by this name, and which I do not as a rule care for.

For all the mystique of fine wine, much hard science and skill in both organisation and method goes into the business. In South Africa the State control is much greater than in France where wines labelled, for instance, Mâcon may well consist of part Mâcon and part Algerian without anybody having the right to complain. This would be unthinkable in South Africa, and the cellar keys are held in duplicate – one by the Company and one by the Excise Office. Another favourable point, of course, is the climate in South Africa, which is always so dependable, a factor which helps greatly in all calculations, especially with regard to the production of brandy.

Quoting from my book on South Africa and my meeting with a then senior Minister in the Government, Mr Paul Sauer, I said:

> Mr Sauer's knowledge of wine, especially South African wine, is vast and all-embracing. For some reason, he regards wine drinkers as cultured folk and beer drinkers as the opposite. 'Those barbarian drinkers of beer' was how he described them to me. In very ancient times, he explained, growers had considered the limit of wines as the Rhine valley in Germany – 'On the other side were barbarians who painted their faces and bodies with woad and drank beer' he said to me, looking into the depths of a Burgundy glass.

On the whole, I found the white wines better than the red out there, but during the whole of my stay, I felt it a privilege to be in such a civilised, wine-loving country.

As the Wine and Food Society grew in numbers and dinners were held in expensive hotels for two or three hundred guests, I came to the conclusion it was impossible to have a first-class dinner cooked for so many people, and the Lucullus Group was formed, limited to twenty-one members. Members of this Group had of course to be elected by other members of the Wine and Food Society. Allegedly, only top gourmets and world-wide authorities on food and drink were selected. Those who came to my dinner the year I was Chairman included Sir Francis Colchester-Wemyss, a gentleman who lived in Cheltenham and one of my favourite authorities on wine. Then there was the head man of Handley Page – Sir Frederick Handley Page. Guests were not allowed, but the Chairman was allowed in exceptional cases to have one guest. I had invited my friend Tom Driberg to be my guest that evening.

My duties as Chairman for the year consisted in choosing the menu and wines – without any concern for the costs of either. I here quote from the *Wine and Food Quarterly* of Spring 1939:

> The Fourth Dinner of the Lucullus Group took place on Thursday, January 19th, 1939, at L'Auberge de France, Piccadilly Circus, London. Mr Gerald Hamilton was in the Chair, and he was responsible for the choice of both the fare and the wines. Twenty other members of the Group were present.
>
> **The Fare:** Le Consommé de Tortue à la Royale; Le Saumon du Shannon à la Gelée de Champagne, Sauce Verte; La Fricassée de Poulet Bordelaise; L'Agneau de Pauillac Rôti au Feu de Sarments; Délices de Prague Florentine; Les Truffes sous la Cendre à la façon du Périgord; La Mousse Glacée Cantonaise; La Corbeille de Fruits; Le Café.
>
> **The Wines:** Oloroso 1845; Montrachet 1929; Château Lafite 1924; Domaine du Chevalier 1920 (en Magnums); Chambertin Clos du Bèze 1919; Moët & Chandon, Dry Imperial 1906; Armagnac Château d'Anthras, 1820; Solera 1842; Grande Fine Champagne 1878 (Reserve Dertu).

I venture to think that the menu could not have been bettered and would like to draw the reader's attention to the dish of truffles. Each small earthenware container held one large truffle, inside was put butter and liqueur brandy, then the cover was pasted round to exclude all air; this was cooked for about twenty-four hours in a slow oven; when each guest opened his little jar, the aroma that filled the room was unforgettable – almost as unforgettable as the taste of the truffles.

One bottle of one of the wines I remember was corked, but that was hardly my fault. Actually the dinner went off very well, except for a little trouble at the very beginning, as the Communist Party had heard this somewhat lavish banquet was about to take place and a crowd of demonstrators besieged the restaurant, bearing banners – 'We are starving and have no work'. When they came up the stairs of the restaurant to the private room, I naturally consented to see them and said that if any member of their party was really hungry, I would be delighted if he or she would be my guest that evening. This offer was not accepted and I then went on to try to explain that a great many of my friends spent large sums of money on buying valuable paintings. I personally had only one weakness and that was my love of food and drink. The comparatively small sum spent on this indulgence was nothing like what other people spent on jewellery and paintings. I had no jewellery and certainly no paintings. Fortunately my frank approach seemed to pacify my unexpected visitors, who retired in good order before the police, for whom the restaurant proprietor had sent, arrived. The newspapers next morning had full accounts of this *contretemps*.

I did not want to have champagne in the middle of the meal, but Graham Moffat, who had helped me choose the wines, said it was rather expected at an English feast. Of course, I personally love champagne and whenever I have the opportunity drink it with joy, but I do not care for it with a meal. When I lived in Paris and champagne was comparatively cheap, I always enjoyed a half-bottle in the middle of the morning and another half-bottle at six or so in the evening. It did me a tremendous amount of good.

The Lucullus dinners, unlike the Memorable Meals rubric in the *Wine and Food Quarterly*, were never discussed as it was supposed that the guests were themselves the best critics and any comment was superfluous. This meal at which I was Chairman may seem exaggeratedly sumptuous, but as a matter of fact in Good King Edward's day similar meals were being served all the time. The only concession made to guests at these meals was that halfway through there was a pause, during which something like a sorbet would be served to give the guest time to recover from what he had already eaten before he attacked the next part of the meal. In German this break was known as a *'Mahlpause'* and was more frequently met with in Germany than in England at the beginning of the century.

I am always partly shocked and partly amazed at watching the wine waiter in English restaurants uncorking a bottle before it has been brought to room temperature, for the host to taste before even the oxygen in the air has had a chance to play its beneficial role in the first few minutes of the bottle being opened. The average English host puts on a knowing look, nods his head to the wine waiter and his unfortunate guests each get a glass of wine which may or may not have been corked (as I have seen happen only the other day).

My articles in *Everybody's* and frequent ones in the *Wine and Food Quarterly* no doubt irritated some readers. I am a great advocate of garlic for example, which I consider to be the most healthy vegetable in existence as it disinfects the stomach and I believe it to be a perfect prophylactic when rheumatism and kindred ailments are involved. Then again, I am shocked by the amount of Ceylon and Indian tea consumed in England. I cannot believe that tea consumed in such large amounts can be good for anybody. The tannin is excessive and dangerous and in England people drink very strong tea on each and every occasion. In France, as my reader probably knows, tea, or an 'infusion', is usually drunk when one is ill. It is true that English habits – tea, whisky, etc – have now reached France, but in my young days no one drank tea there as they do in England. I have not included China tea, as this is a most delicious beverage properly served at the right strength and with lemon. But I can only say I have no tea in the house – not even China tea – as the whole idea of 'Afternoon Tea' frightens me. The digestive rhythm between lunch and dinner is destroyed.

In another chapter I have referred to my reluctance ever to drink water, although in my own house I keep Malvern Water in the refrigerator and when in France prefer *Eau de Vittel* to any other. I consider tap water not only unhealthy but dangerous in view of all the chemicals which admittedly are added to the water at the waterworks. In this connection I remember a dinner in Madrid when I was dining with Prince Nicholas of Rumania, and I refused water. He agreed with me and announced to the guests that he himself never allowed any tap water to touch his lips.

Rather impishly I said to him in French, the language we were speaking, 'But, sir, how do you manage to clean your teeth then?' He immediately replied, '*Ah, pour me laver les dents j'ai un petit vin blanc tout spécial.*' I was so delighted to hear this, because it seemed that after all the Royal families of Europe had not entirely forgotten their reputation for decadence.

Chapter Fourteen

The Press

I KNOW IT is the custom of many writers to blame the press. My own experience of the press, with one exception which will be described later, has been a very happy one. At one time I used to feed the William Hickey column in the *Daily Express* with paragraphs, sometimes when Tom Driberg was in charge of that column and, before I went to live in Spain, when John Ellison edited it.

An old friend of mine from Berlin days in the early thirties was Claud Cockburn. I liked him very much, as I admired his erudition and his aplomb in dealing with unpleasant situations. An opportunity occurred for me to do him a kindness when his auto-biography appeared some years ago, as I was reviewing books for the *Spectator* at the time and I persuaded the then literary editor, Iain Hamilton, to allow me to do a long review of this book and to give it pride of place in that particular issue of the *Spectator*. This he kindly arranged and I wrote a long article, praising the book. The article appeared under the title 'Claud in Clover' in the *Spectator* of 24th February 1956. When I next chanced to meet Claud he thanked me very profusely for what he called my kindness and said he thought my article would certainly help the sale of his book.

When Cockburn's autobiography was published as a paperback, I naturally did not take the trouble to get it or read it, as I had read it very thoroughly when reviewing it. To my horror friends telephoned me saying I should take action against Cockburn and Penguin Books Ltd for what he had said about me. Cockburn had inserted in the paperback edition a great deal about me and very much against me. He said, for instance, that I had introduced him in Paris to a famous armaments manufacturer who wished Cockburn to do some work for him. The fact that I have never in my whole life met an armaments manufacturer seemed beside the point. He also said I was going to marry the mistress or the daughter of the said armaments manufacturer. He gave neither name nor address – or any other detail – of this tycoon and most readers of his book naturally did not credit this story.

It seems so odd to me that anybody should express his gratitude to me for the kindness I had done in such a manner. It is true that I did not have any disagreeable repercussions from his statements, as perhaps his book was not very much read, but it might have been a catastrophe for me, not possessing the means to start an expensive libel action.

My friend Robin Maugham approached me because he wanted to write a series of several articles about me for a Sunday newspaper. These articles were not to be complimentary, but he informed me that the Editor of the paper had offered him a substantial sum for these articles. I said I would help him and would not mind what he said, if I could read his articles first, and expect to receive half the sum mentioned. But not a bit of it. Very foolishly, but needing money (as has often been the case with me in recent years), I consented to accept a much smaller fee. The articles were sensational – so much so that at the time they were being written the famous train robbery case was in all the papers and the then Editor telephoned Robin Maugham, who was in Madrid with me at the time, saying they must have some reference to a train robbery. When Maugham answered that as far as he knew I had never had anything to do with a train robbery, the Editor said, 'Oh, let him think back and he might remember some such occasion!'

As I conclude this chapter, I am shocked to hear of the death of my friend Bob Pitman at the early age of forty-four. This journalist has always shown me great kindness and consideration, and I am happy to have been his guest on one or two occasions at his house at Twickenham, which he changed for another house at Shepperton shortly before his death. I am particularly grateful to him for the encouragement he gave me and for his very flattering review of my book *Blood Royal* in the *Sunday Express*.

Hardly have I written about my friend Bob Pitman, when the news comes, as I write, of Kingsley Martin's death in Cairo. Of all the journalists I have ever met, he was the most intriguing and I am told very demanding to work for, but obviously very capable, since he brought the *New Statesman*'s circulation up to such a high level. I first met him when I lived in Paris after the First World War and came over to London occasionally. If I remember right, he seemed to have luncheon parties each Monday at the Red Lion inn near his offices. He was kind enough to invite me to these when I was in England. At these luncheons I met a number of interesting journalists: Richard Crossman for instance, Leonard Woolf, Negley Farson, and others. The conversation at these luncheons was brilliant, erudite and political, but unfortunately the food at the Red Lion was not then up to this standard.

Readers may wonder at my affection for the *New Statesman*, which is a notoriously left-wing publication and especially as I worked for some years as a book reviewer for the rival weekly *The Spectator*. The reason is I admire the sincerity and the logic of the contributors and more than this I admire the perfect English in which these articles were written. Furthermore, the *New Statesman* has always shown tremendous fairness and readily publishes letters, sometimes by myself, disagreeing with a great deal. I did not see much of Kingsley Martin recently, except at parties; at one given by Anthony Blond I was able to have a long talk with him – this must have been about five years ago. The last time I saw Kingsley Martin was when I was cashing a cheque at Coutts' Bank in the Strand recently and he came in by chance and stood by me at the same counter. He remembered me well and we had a brief chat. My recollection of him is that he was an asset socially, but a terrible pessimist.

Chapter Fifteen

Memories

As I WRITE this book so many incidents, and I might say adventures, occur to me which can be put under no particular heading. Here are some of them:

A rather eccentric but very erudite clergyman who was chaplain at Bristol Prison met me in London several times, and I was surprised one day to get a letter from him asking whether I would be prepared to give a lecture to the prisoners at the prison he attended. This was accompanied by a note from the then Governor, who is no doubt still the Governor, supporting this request.

This was at a time when my second autobiography had just appeared and was much commented on in the press. It was pointed out that the Home Office would no doubt cover the expenses of my journey, but that there would be no fee attached. A day was fixed and so I journeyed down to Bristol and stayed at a hotel, where the kind chaplain had reserved accommodation for me. He came and had lunch with me at the hotel and in the evening took me to the prison. I thought to myself I would find time during the train journey to think about what I was going to talk on, but with my usual tendency to put things off, I arrived at Bristol station without a single thought as to what I was going to say.

The Church of England chapel was used as a lecture hall, a curtain being drawn across the altar, and upon the platform was the Governor, myself and the chaplain. Row by row the prisoners entered the chapel, each row accompanied by a warder. The chaplain introduced me and, still wondering what I was going to say, I stood up and said:

> I hear you fellows recently were subjected to a lecture on the habits of fishes which did not go down very well. As I am not a very clever man and I do not know much about many things, I think it is as well to give you a lecture about myself, because that is a subject I really know something about.

I spoke then of my autobiography and related various incidents, amusing and adventurous, that had happened to me. After half-an-hour of the lecture, there was another half-hour set aside for the prisoners to ask me any questions they liked, and I was genuinely surprised at the most intelligent questions put to me. At the time of my lecture there was a great deal of publicity about Anna Andersen, who claimed to be the Grand Duchess Anastasia of Russia and who was then living in Germany. It happened that I knew a little about this matter and had actually seen this lady. I was, therefore, able to assure my audience that she most certainly was not the Grand Duchess, but that having been recognised as such by various highly placed Royal persons and not being a very intelligent woman, she sincerely thought by this time she really was the Czar's daughter.

This reminded me very much of the Tichborne claimant's case when an impostor managed to get himself recognised by the baronet's mother as her son. In view of the adulation he received at first, he ended by genuinely believing he was Sir Roger Tichborne. One or two other prisoners got up to say that they were entirely innocent of any offence and their condemnation was a put-up job. I had to be very tactful in these cases and say that I could hardly help them in these matters or else I might not be able to get out of the prison at all that evening. This silly pleasantry went down very well. The Governor thanked me for a very interesting and harmonious lecture. I use the word harmonious because other lecturers had apparently been hissed and booed. I had dinner as the chaplain's guest at a very charming hotel and returned to London the following morning.

The first time I went to America after the Second World War I went by sea and my first business after arriving in New York was to go to Washington to see certain people about the matters which took me across the Atlantic. In 1947 or '48 when this journey took place, it was customary on reaching Washington station to share the large taxis with other travellers, the taxi driver setting down his clients each at the address he wanted to go to. This was a pleasant and cheap arrangement, especially as the Americans in the taxi made friends with each other and with me in the space of a few minutes. When I had occasion to go from New York to Boston later on, I hurried towards a taxi, into which a very distinguished elderly gentleman had just stepped, and hearing him give the same name of the street as my hotel, I jumped in, though I did not receive a welcoming smile at all. Knowing how friendly Americans are I thought I would introduce myself and said, 'My name is Hamilton'; the companion in my taxi turned to me and simply said, 'And mine is not.' It was only then I realised that the custom which obtained at Washington station did not obtain at Boston, and I was much chaffed when I got to the hotel, in view of the importance of the gentleman whose taxi I had shared – his chauffeur and car not having been at the station.

I had an introduction to Colonel McCormick, the proprietor of the *Chicago Tribune*, and when I was in Chicago I presented my letter of introduction. A day later a gentleman named Jung called on me and took me to lunch. He must have given a satisfactory report about me to the Colonel as the Colonel himself gave me an appointment for a day or two later. While waiting in the ante-chamber at his office, members of his staff kept coming in to look at me and making remarks such as, 'It's a great honour that the Colonel wishes to see you – he hates Britishers' – and then, 'Whatever you do, don't make any jokes when you see the Colonel, he doesn't like pleasantries.' Finally, the doors opened and the most enormous dog I have ever seen came out sniffing, and the Colonel behind the dog. I got on very well with Colonel Mc-Cormick and he invited me to spend the weekend at his country place at Whateley. I duly arrived on the afternoon I was expected and was taken to my room and later the guests were assembled for dinner. Drinks were handed round and consumed with great enjoyment, but I was very careful to take only one whisky as I thought, 'I am in the house of a multi-millionaire and the wines at dinner are sure to be superb and all will be spoilt if I take more than one whisky.' But not at all; I sat on Mrs McCormick's left and all I saw on the table was iced water. When the coloured man-servant kept offering it to me, I always put my hand over my glass, hoping something more interesting would be offered me. Mrs McCormick, noticing what I did, said, 'Don't you like water, Mr Hamilton?' I replied, 'Yes indeed, to wash in, but not to drink', and she asked if I would like something else, so I most modestly asked if there was any beer in the house as I would like to have some. Fortunately, her cooks were German and insisted on beer with their meals, so there was plenty. A can was brought to me and deposited in front of me. Later, with the coffee, every kind of drink was offered but no wine ever, and it is wine that I need more than spirits or other drinks. Some time after, I saw the Colonel in Tangier when he was on a world tour and I happened to be there, and he reminded me of this incident, about which his wife had told him. He was staying at the Minzah Hotel and calling the head waiter as we were having lunch, told him to bring a bottle of the very best claret the hotel possessed. It happened to be a Mouton-Rothschild of a good vintage year and I felt that amends had been made most honourably.

Whilst I was in Chicago a lady friend rang me up at Palmer House where I was staying and after a brief talk suddenly said, 'Good-bye, Hun.' I thought this must be an allusion to my alleged pro-German sentiments and felt rather hurt. Later, it dawned on me that this was a common expression and short for 'honey' – a term really of endearment. Another event in Chicago at first puzzled me and afterwards amused me. I had had dinner at a first-class restaurant with a famous stock-broker and his wife and after dinner he went to get his car and I stayed in the hall of the restaurant looking for my hostess. On enquiry I was told she had gone to the rest room. 'Goodness,' I said, 'is she so tired?' – only then did it dawn on me that this was the American equivalent of the silly English expression the 'cloakroom'. I was very happy in Chicago and really liked that town better than New York.

I even went on to Kansas City to be the guest of honour at the inaugural dinner of the Kansas City Wine & Food Society. I had to make a speech and did so, blaming America for the three greatest set-backs that the wine trade has ever suffered from – the phylloxera bug which ruined the vineyards of France of course came from America; the vile cocktail habit also started in America; and last, but I suppose not least, prohibition was also first practised in that country. The Americans seemed to like this attack and I was loudly cheered.

I first was taken to America by my father before the First World War when I was but a small boy and it was at the time of the Delhi Durbar, which was of great interest to Americans because, as is well known, Lord Curzon, the then Viceroy of India, had married a Chicago lady – Miss Leiter, the daughter of Zacharias Leiter, a millionaire store magnate. I remember one picture was published, amidst descerptions of the grandeur of the ceremonies and so on, of the low-bowing rajahs with the heading: 'Old Zach's daughter makes 'em bend'.

On another occasion, when in California, a coloured revivalist minister named Jeremiah Johnson had been accused of the rape of a white lady and was sentenced to death. This sentence was carried out and there was great publicity in the newspapers. The clever pressmen found a suitable heading even for this grim occasion – one paper said: 'Jeremiah Jerked to Jesus'.

Just before the First World War started I had made the acquaintance of Harry Pilcer, who was an American and one of the leading lights of the music-hall stage in London. I met him originally through Gaby Deslys, whom I knew quite well, and they were appearing together in a review at the Palace Theatre which I frequently attended. When, as usual in autumn, I went abroad for the winter, I let my beautiful London home to Harry Pilcer.

Apparently quarrels never ceased between him and Gaby Deslys, who lived in Albert Hall Mansions at the time, and the cause of the jealousy was that great artist Basil Hallam. Finally, Harry and Gaby broke off their attachment and when I returned from abroad I determined to bring them together again. I got Harry into one room and Gaby in another, without each knowing the other was in the house, and finally, after I had spoken to both of them and I thought the moment ripe, I asked Harry to come into the room where Gaby was – and shut the door firmly on them – and they thus made up their differences.

Gaby Deslys was, as is well known, alleged to have been kept at this time by Gordon Selfridge, whom I also knew well and liked tremendously. My own opinion is that his friendship for Gaby was really a typical American advertising stunt, because she used to visit the store (I think every Wednesday in the week) and shoppers from the provinces and suburbs were able to watch this elegant lady making her purchases and they whispered to each other – 'Of course, you know she is kept by Mr Gordon Selfridge.' What is so amusing is that very few people seem to know that Gaby Deslys, the most French of all soubrettes at the time, was not a French-woman at all; she was an Austrian who had only learned the French language comparatively recently. I have always found something very tragic and very depressing in the lives of these great international beauties. I do not believe any of them know real happiness – as a happily married young bourgeois couple so often do.

The news of the recent death of my dear friend Tallulah Bankhead came as a shock to me. Friends of hers all seemed to think that she would last for ever. Her kindnesses and her thoughtfulness towards her friends is one of the most unforgettable features of her compli-cated character. I got to know her originally through her sister, Eugenia, whom I first met in Tangier.

Whenever Tallulah – whom I used to call, like certain other of her friends, Talloo – came to London latterly she always stayed at the Ritz and many a time and oft have I visited here there. One of the last times was when she was in the middle of a feud with Nancy Spain. The latter had written an article for the *Daily Express* about Tallulah, who had insisted on being allowed to read the article before it was published. Unfortunately, Nancy omitted to show Tallulah her article which appeared with many comments Tallulah objected to. I arrived about five that afternoon and was almost knocked over by a fleeing Nancy who said, 'I can't stop, I can't stop'. I went up to Tallulah's apartment and found her in a towering rage, with a broken vase at her feet which she had apparently thrown at Nancy. I managed to soothe her a little and suddenly had a brain-wave. I said to her, 'My dear, you've very fond of poetry, do you happen to remember these lines:

Sink me the ship, Master Gunner – sink her, split her in twain!
Fall into the hands of God, not into the hands of Spain!'

This amused Tallulah, who wrote me a very nice letter thanking me for cheering her up with this quotation.

On another occasion she came down from her apartment and met me in the foyer of the Ritz, where tea was just being served. The waiter asked if he should bring tea for two and Talloo said, 'I don't want any tea; I would like some champagne.' The foreign waiter produced the head waiter who very politely said they could not serve champagne in the public rooms until about 5.30, and suggested that if she went upstairs to her suite, as a resident she could be served there. Talloo was most indignant and said she was not a piece on a chess board to be moved about when she was thirsty, and when the waiter reiterated that he could not serve her, she called out very loudly, 'Go and telephone to the head of police in this bloody country and say a poor decrepit American actress wants a glass of champagne.' These instructions were not carried out, but the manager and the head waiter went into a huddle and finally a large ewer arrived and into tea-cups was poured an excellent (non-vintage) Bollinger.

A lot has been said about her calling everybody 'Darling'. Actually, her pronunciation of the word was unlike anybody else's and was really 'Dolling'. It was no great honour to be called this by her, since she used the expression indiscriminately to waiters and saleswomen in shops as well as her friends. The only other person I know in England who calls everybody darling – but he pronounces it 'Daharling' – is Mr Robert Morley, who recently on television, disagreeing with Mary Stokes, gave her more 'Daharlings' than I expect she has had for a very long time.

As a very young man I was tremendously impressed by the wonderful poetry of Algernon Swinburne. When I grew up, rather to my surprise I found that Swinburne was still alive and living in Putney as the house guest of Walter Watts-Dunton. I wrote to this gentleman in order to say how honoured I would be if the great Poet ever had time to see me. Rather to my surprise I received a letter from Mr Watts-Dunton saying that the Poet would be pleased to see me on a certain day a week or two ahead, and I was to call at 'The Pines' on Putney Hill at about four o'clock. It was a very hot summer's day as my hansom ascended Putney Hill and the clip-clop of the horse's hooves matched the grumbling of the hansom driver. Finally, however, we reached 'The Pines' and I paid the cabby lavishly for his efforts, expressing my sorrow for his trusty horse. When I rang the bell, a trim maid ushered me in and I entered a room where I found Mr Watts-Dunton seated in a comfortable chair with several books in front of him and with an enormous eye shade over both his eyes. Conversation seemed a bit stilted. Tea was brought, the inevitable accompaniment of an afternoon in England, and Mr Watts-Dunton began to question me about my love of poetry and what I intended to do in life. He asked if I wished to take up a literary career; I said laughingly, 'Oh, nothing as violent as that!' – a remark which did not seem to go down very well.

While we were talking, there were footsteps in the room above us and I heard the occupant of the room impatiently walking up and down. I knew this must be Swinburne himself – the caged lion of Putney. After some desultory conversation I was more than ever anxious to meet the Poet, but unfortunately I had evidently not passed the acid test required of visitors to the presence of the

Poet. I had been too flippant in my replies to the questions put to me and so, after a short interval, Mr Watts-Dunton rose and said it was a great pity the Poet was not very well today and for that reason wondered if I would be able to apply to see him in a few months' time when his health would, no doubt, be better. I, of course, agreed and tried to hide my disappointment. Again the footsteps above my head reminded me that the imprisoned lion was no doubt as anxious to come down as I was to see him, but his keeper was adamant and I gracefully withdrew, searching in vain for a hansom to take me home.

After the passage of a few months I was busy concocting a second letter, hoping the Poet was better and would have time to meet me. When I went out to post the letter the evening papers bore the announcement of the sudden death of the great poet Algernon Swinburne. This saved me a penny stamp, but I felt very angry with Mr Watts-Dunton who was censor and keeper of one of the greatest poets England has ever known.

Long, long ago, and well before the First World War, some of the friends of Oscar Wilde used to meet in a Soho restaurant, which no longer exists, called 'Trevigilo'. I, of course, never knew Wilde, but every Sunday when we met, old More Adey, who had been a great friend of Wilde, acted as host. Amongst those who came was Christopher Millard, who on two or three occasions brought Robbie Ross to the party. I met the latter several times, but never knew him very well.

Bosie Douglas was of course absent from these gatherings, for, although I knew him well, this was at the time there were lawsuits between him and Robbie Ross. I have written so much about my long friendship with Douglas that I will not refer to this any more, since other books of mine contain an account of our frequent journeys to Paris and my trips to Brighton, where his old mother, Lady Queensberry, lived and died. Bosie, too, died near Brighton at Lancing.

Every time I go to the Cadogan Hotel, I am always reminded of Betjeman's magnificent poem entitled *The Arrest of Oscar Wilde*, which took place in that most respectable hotel. Quite recently, an American friend of mine, a great bore, not having been able to get into the Carlton Towers Hotel, crossed the road and took a room at the Cadogan Hotel. He invited me to lunch one day and over the lunch table said, almost in a whisper, 'I have something to tell you, Gerald, I don't suppose you know it – Oscar Wilde was arrested in this very hotel where we are sitting!'

'Good God,' I replied. 'Whatever for?'

Index

143